My Grandmother Stole Hubcaps

Toni Emmons

Copyright © 2022 Toni Emmons

All rights reserved.

ISBN: 9798433488069

No part of this publication may be reproduced, stored in a retrieval system, or transmitted in any form or by any means- electronic, mechanical, photocopy, recording, or otherwise without written permission from the author.
Email contact: authort.emmons01@gmail.com

This story is my truth, perception of facts, and personal experience with a battle no one chooses. In addition, the things found within these pages are not diagnostic tools or treatment recommendations.

Cover Design by Bianca Brown
www.iambiancabrown.com

Editing by A.T. Destiny Awaits Group LLC
atdestinyawaitsgroup@gmail.com

DEDICATION

I dedicate this book to Grandmom, and I pray that she found the peace in death that she never found in life. Also, to the families and caregivers who have already taken or will take this journey in the future, may you find hope and peace.

CONTENTS

Acknowledgments...................................vi

Introduction...1

My Grandmother Stole Hubcaps..6

Mental Health is a Team Sport..16

Getting to Know Grandmom..22

Don't Forget Your Company Manners...36

Grandmom's a Vampire.......................44

Dementia, not Alzheimer's....................49

Quirks and Clues................................57

Conversations with Dead Relatives........69

Being Forgotten...................................75

Pick Your Battles................................81

Pouring from an Empty Cup..................97

We Need Help! Now What?....................108

Opinions, Everybody Has One.............117

Grief Cycle..124

About the Author................................130

Thank You

Thank you to my amazing husband, Jerad. I love you and am blessed to have you as my person. Thank you for putting up with all of my shenanigans.

Thank you to my massive and wacky family. I am so blessed for our chaotic mess, and I wouldn't have it any other way!

Last but not least, Que Nona Guilford, THANK YOU for holding my hand and helping me get out of my own way. I could not have done this without your support and prayers. I love you, and I am grateful for you.

Welcome to My Journey

Thank you for taking the time to share this journey with me. It is a generational story involving three generations of a family struggling through mental health and Dementia. We are just a regular family. But that is where the beauty in the story lies. Our battle is happening to families all over, and each one will be unique.

This story isn't a happy one. There will not be a miraculous, heartwarming ending. Spoiler alert! My Grandmother died, and the last few years were frequently hell on earth for her. She was lost and frightened, often unable to understand what was happening to her and around her. I cannot imagine how Grandmom must have felt spending every day surrounded by strangers that looked so similar to people she once knew but couldn't place. Dementia is not a disease that only impacts the person living with it. The person with Dementia pays a heartbreaking price, and so do their loved ones.

Grandmom wasn't a bad person, nor a saint, and she could be incredibly loving and cruel in a span of a few minutes. She was simply human, with often untreated mental health problems, personality quirks, and a flare for the dramatic. I loved her very much. But she was what I describe, kindly, as difficult.

I firmly believe she was aware of a decline long before we figured out how far the disease had progressed. Grandmom was scary smart; she only went to school through the 8th grade and was still one of the most intelligent people I ever met. Once she realized she was becoming forgetful, the steps she took to hide that fact from others were extraordinary, in my opinion. I view this as a testament to the complexity of the human mind and how past experiences and beliefs impact cognitive decline. We only began to see atypical problems once she stopped noticing that she was forgetting. I stopped blaming us for not seeing signs sooner a long time ago.

Near the end of Grandmom's life, there were often new obstacles and challenges to face. Some of the events and situations we found ourselves in were humorous, some frightening, and some sad. Every emotion I could imagine played out in rapid-fire real-time. Grandmom needed full-time support at the end. Yet she responded negatively to immediate family members.

She was many things to many people, and there is no way to cover all of them in a single book. Perhaps it is best to think of this as a highlight reel, focusing on a sad and challenging time in her life and mine. Grandmom's cognitive difficulties during Dementia and her lifelong mental health struggles may or may not have had an association. In addition to that, some of her quirks were cultural or generational. And some of the things she did were just a part of who she was and were simply personality oddities. The many areas covered within these pages play into the battle she fought with mental health and cognitive decline.

In this story, you may find that I am the bad guy or at least a little bit of a bully, and I am okay with that. I made choices that were not always right and pushed hard for things that my mother needed more time to accept. All of my family handled my Grandmom's battle with Dementia differently, and each of us perceived events and coped differently. I have a large family, but in this tale, when I talk of Grandmom's immediate family, this includes me, my oldest brother, my mom, and Mom's sister. Any references to the extended family include a host of cousins, Grandmom's brothers and sisters, and any in-laws.

This book does not have answers for dealing with Dementia or grief. However, I want to believe that our struggle will give others hope. I do not think that there is a generic form of this disease or a one-size-fits-all approach to handling the challenges that come with it. In addition, the things found within these pages are not diagnostic tools or treatment recommendations. This story is my truth, perception of facts, and personal experience with a battle no one chooses.

There are events and situations that I find humorous. Humor is my default; I look for the silver lining rather than the sadness. I believe Grandmom's lifelong battle with depression and sadness contributed to developing my default emotion. I have been called names and told I was making fun of Grandmom's Dementia battle. Dementia is not a laughing matter, and I am not making fun of Grandmom. My promise to you, the reader, is Grandmom would have seen the humor in these same events on her good days. The reality of caring for a loved one with Dementia is mostly a heartbreaking, no-win scenario. Yet, some of the situations we found ourselves in were funny. I believe life is hard but generally funny, and we have to find the silver lining within it or risk spending our lives crying.

During this process, I have laughed, cried, and been angry, and I will be honored if you choose to participate in those feelings with me. Writing has been a healing process, and I have had moments to remember my love for a highly complex woman. It has brought me peace to share Grandmom with you.

If you are reading this, I hope you find comfort in knowing that there is no correct way to deal with Dementia. As a caregiver, you are not alone. Your struggles, anger, laughter, exhaustion, grief, and other emotions that take over your mind are all valid. Know that cognitive decline is also not a battle our loved ones would have picked for themselves, and no one comes out as a winner. Ideally, the loved one and the caregiver maintain a positive quality of life and mental health until the end. I hope reading this uplifts your quality of life, mental health, or outlook. May there be some peace along the journey.

My Grandmother Stole Hubcaps

My Grandmother stole hubcaps, or at least one. Yes, you read that correctly, and I am not the least bit ashamed that she did. She loved "all things" shiny. I found it funny then and still find it funny. The stories around her tendency towards minor theft often elicit shocked responses.

"How could you not know something was wrong?"

"Why didn't you say something?"

"That is so out of character?"

I always found those questions dripped with judgment. Perhaps those asking the questions could benefit from loosening up? Conceivably I have an odd sense of humor? Or maybe you just had to be there and live through the situation? The truth is sometimes you must find the humor in life, or you will spend all of your time crying. Looking back at the last twenty years of her life, stealing the hubcap was one of several situations that demonstrated cognitive decline. However, it also indicated that she was getting sick of her neighbor's parking. So, it wasn't the tremendous clue people tend to think it was.

Grandmom's progression through Dementia impacted rationalization, impulse control, and the ability to process environmental surroundings and situations. Grandmom was living with Dementia, but her declining mental state affected the whole family. Seeing a loved one's actions versus personally processing and understanding a loved one's decline are different tasks. There is an abundance of advice on dealing with your loved one's disease and how to make decisions for them. Too often, well-meaning family, friends, and even strangers will tell you all of the ways you are failing your loved one. However, when dealing with the human brain, the uniqueness of this problem, their individual lives, and lived experiences will make it challenging in a manner that defies imagination. It is a lot! So, for now, let's start with the hubcap.

In Virginia's coal country, the roads are winding and often riddled with potholes and various road hazards. Losing and finding hubcaps along the roadside is an expected part of driving in that region. My stepdad lost a hubcap on his truck a few months prior and had difficulty finding a matching replacement. However, it was not a pressing matter.

During a visit with my grandmother, she noticed the missing hubcap. Grandmom had always found incomplete sets bothersome, especially if a clearly defined number was required. For example, only having three out of four irritated her. Of course, during the visit, Grandmom noticed and mentioned the missing hubcap. An innocuous conversation followed in which Grandmom said she would watch out for one. A relatively benign conversation over something that wasn't a big deal and honestly just an uneventful, common situation under most circumstances.

Soon after, Grandmom contacted my stepdad, saying she had found a perfect hubcap for his truck. He was a little surprised that after months a hubcap just turned up. Making conversation, he asked where she found it? Her response was vague; she just found it and didn't remember exactly where. He didn't press the issue. He knew she became defensive and easier to upset these days. It was best to accept the gift and not push her because to continue to question her would result in a fight. He now had a replacement hubcap, and life moved on.

A short time later, I was home for a visit and went to see Grandmom. I noticed her neighbor parked along the street very close to her driveway as I was leaving. According to Grandmom, the neighbor frequently parked too close to her driveway, and she wasn't happy with that. Funny thing, though, the neighbor's truck was almost identical to my stepdad's truck. It was a similar year, the same size but different color. And what do you know? It had the same hubcaps. Well, the remaining three were the same. I walked around the truck, and the neighbor just happened to be missing the hubcap on the wheel closest to Grandmom's driveway. I stood in the driveway dumbfounded. Had I just discovered where Grandmom found the hubcap?

I started to laugh and not just a little chuckle. I was bent over with tears streaming down my face, busting a gut laughing. The absurdity of the situation was more than I could process at that moment, and I could do nothing but laugh. Until I realized that if the neighbors saw me in my fit of mirth, it might raise questions. I hurried into my car and continued laughing as I drove to Mom's house.

So why am I telling you that Grandmom most likely stole the neighbor's hubcap? Because we laughed about it and decided not to fight that battle over what may have happened. Perhaps she didn't remember where she found it. But even if she remembered, she would never have admitted to finding it out front, possibly knowing the owner, and making a choice not to return the hubcap. She was very concerned with what others thought of her, and choosing to keep the hubcap would have reflected poorly.

Knowing my Grandmom, the neighbor kept parking too close to her driveway. Grandmom seriously did not like how the neighbor parked and frequently complained about his parking skills or lack of skills. Her impulse control was diminished enough that she could see nothing wrong with taking the hubcap; after all, my stepdad needed one. And have I mentioned Grandmom always had some passive-aggressive tendencies? Grandmom worked very hard to keep the mischievous streak hidden. Still, it became harder to hide those tendencies. She would express a desire to do or say things to others but seldom acted on those desires. The concern for how others viewed her and perceived expectations controlled her. Additionally, the ability to rationalize and evaluate right from wrong prevented her from acting on her impulses. As Grandmom's Dementia progressed, the ability to refrain from these impulses declined.

Even if Grandmom found the hubcap near her house, not asking the neighbor first or deciding not to return the hubcap were both outside her typical behaviors. The rationale behind the choice was questionable, and questioning the decision would have resulted in a fight. I quickly learned how to avoid fighting with her because she tended to be ruthless even before Dementia when she was angry. As her cognitive function declined, anger became her default, and she could be cruel when angry.

Grandmom did many things that others would view as out of character. For us, the only thing atypical about it was she did it where others would judge her for it and did not seem to care. Also, her inhibitions declined with Dementia. For us, Grandmom taking the item herself was the odd part.

Grandmom had always been a bit of a thief. Or at least a thief enabler, she may not have stolen the item, but she orchestrated the theft. Her penchant for thievery may not be what immediately comes to mind for many people. I certainly didn't know I was stealing when she put me out of the car to collect a pretty rock beside the road. But come to find out, it is illegal to take stones and vegetation from government-owned land. After learning that, I realized I was a serial criminal.

Grandmom loved rocks and had a large rock garden filled with pretty stones from every place she visited. Many of these stones she loved so well came from sites you are not supposed to remove rocks or plants, like the state forest. And there I was, her dastardly little sidekick joyously helping to gather up our ill-gotten gains. I will not lie and pretend that those adventures were anything other than fun. I had a blast when we were stealing rocks.

Grandmom adored pretty, glimmery things and decorated her world with them. The older she got, the brighter and bolder the things became. The love of sparkly things remained a consistent aspect of her Dementia. Her home was full of decorative items that sparkled, and the outside was the same. Grandmom filled the rock garden with suncatchers and decorated the fence from end to end; the flashier, the better. As Grandmom got older, she wore more jewelry. She loved bracelets, and the more sparkle, the better. I am sure I inherited this from her because my favorite color is shiny. However, I usually confine my shiny obsession to nail polish or jewelry at this point in my life.

After Grandmom moved into assisted living, she did not have a lot of her sparkly jewelry. But we tried to include sparkly decorations from her house into her tiny apartment. Soon after the move, Mom received a call from the facility notifying her that Grandmom had begun taking the salt and pepper shakers from the dining room. They asked Mom to come and retrieve them.

Mom arrived at the facility to gather up the shakers, only to find they were identical to the salt and pepper shaker collection at Grandmom's house. Grandmom kept about five sets on a silver tray in the entertainment center at her house. When asked why she kept them there, she said she just liked them. They were cut like crystal with a sparkly silver top, and Grandmom felt the shakers were too pretty for use.

Mom explained how they looked like the ones Grandmom owned. When Mom checked the apartment, it was easy to locate Grandmom's little stash of shakers. It seems, Grandmom collected a new set at each meal in the facility and took them back to her room. I still chuckle at this memory. I get it, she thought they were her property, and I can imagine what she thought of someone using those shakers. The abstract idea that multiple people could own a similar item became increasingly difficult. She believed the shakers belonged to her; she recognized something familiar and took it to her apartment. The idea that the facility could own similar shakers was preposterous. This situation became an agree, redirect, and move-on process while avoiding debate about the ownership as much as possible.

The people at the facility were not upset about the missing shakers. It was a little inconvenient during a meal when they were short. However, as professionals, they recognized the behavior as a regular part of transitioning into a new environment and the change in her ability to process information. The combined knowledge of the professionals who deal with the daily behaviors associated with cognitive decline is necessary for families. The support and reassurance from the professionals in this environment were a benefit to our family. While I believe no two people will act identically during the progression through Dementia, some behaviors frequently occur from person to person. Having an outside source to help identify these behaviors is essential. Additionally, something out of character for the loved one may be one of these more common traits. Knowing this and keeping this in mind can help navigate the changes we will see and the changes they will experience.

Analyzing the behaviors and identifying if it is something to be concerned over versus usual changing preferences only comes after the fact. I can see the patterns and evolution now, years after Grandmom's death, but they were not as easy to see, during those final years. I have had to forgive myself for not identifying the patterns soon enough to prevent some things from happening.

A lifetime ago, I worked in a field where

finding patterns and trends was my thing. I also have an Associate Degree as an Occupational Therapy Assistant. Technically, I have a background that should have helped me identify some of Grandmom's behavioral trends. But when it came to Grandmom and my own family, I had difficulty seeing what was happening. I find that is one of the more challenging aspects of dealing with Dementia. No matter how prepared, how well-versed in the disease, and how much knowledge or experience with others, our perception of things changes when it becomes personal. And that is perfectly fine. I have learned it is okay to make the best worst decision in a no-win situation. There is no perfect solution to dealing with Dementia, and there are no correct answers. We do the best we can to improve our quality of life and our loved one's quality of life as long as possible.

Mental Health is a Team Sport

The stigma surrounding mental health is so strange to me. Your brain controls every other aspect of your body, so why do we think it is acceptable to set aside brain health. We are compassionate to people with touchable and seeable brain conditions such as tumors, clots, or injuries. So why do we disregard those concerns that are not visible on a scan but impact how we live? With all the information available, we still have a stigma around mental wellbeing. Even as I expound on the importance of mental health, I acknowledge that I am part of the suck-it-up and get-over-it generation. I tend to set aside my mental and emotional condition. I have only begun to evaluate its importance as I have internally addressed Grandmom's impact on me and my life outlook.

Since the 1950s, we have made great strides as a society, but we seem to be stuck with the idea that the person can choose or disregard mental health problems. It simply does not work that way! Grandmom's mental health struggles developed as a young woman. Imagine what seeking help was like in the 50s and

60s, but she tried. Grandmom sought help and received treatment from at least one psychologist. Even though Grandmom sought help, it remained a big family secret. No one outside of a few specific family members knew she was seeking treatment. Her sisters denied she ever sought treatment, refusing to acknowledge she spent a month in a psychiatric hospital. Perhaps her sisters did not know about the treatment. Their denial of her depression bothered me tremendously. But that too may be a cultural or generational inconsistency. Her sisters and women in their age group seemed to think that problems magically disappeared if they pretended, they weren't there.

The stigma and avoidance mindset created a situation where mental health treatment for Grandmom only existed during therapy sessions. Our family comes from the Appalachian region. I grew up hearing the prevailing belief that life was hard all over and no one cared about your whining. It isn't an incorrect statement, but it created a culture where we do not openly discuss problems outside of family or a few close friends. But this is not the healthiest belief system and places responsibility for each person's life or expectations on their shoulders. Don't get me wrong, accepting responsibility for our personal lives and actions is a part of growing up. Still, it negates the importance of support systems that humans need. Like it or not, we are communal beings, and we all need a support system. Grandmom did not have an external support system available to receive help outside of therapy sessions. Even within our family, the only time Grandmom mentioned mental health was concerning her Valium prescription. I cannot imagine the additional stress created by a lack of professional support and community secrecy. She had issues everyone could see, but it was all a big secret. It was like, stuff the skeleton in a closet and pretend it does not exist! After all, that always works out so well.

When it came to Grandmom's depression, it was dismissed as "all in her head" more often than it should have been. When I was younger, I failed to realize how condescending and redundant this statement is. Of course, depression was in her head; our brains control emotional states. It's in your head is the biggest copout, non-answer there is for addressing emotional and mental health. As I look back at her life, I am beginning to see how the cycle of depression and anxiety kept repeating. Her inability to break free, even with attempts at treatment, becomes more apparent.

Grandmom's depressive episodes could

often mimic symptoms of Dementia. Telling a doctor that you are experiencing forgetfulness and anxiety can be included in various possible diagnoses. I have had to list these symptoms after an injury that resulted in a lengthy recovery period; the constant pain impacted some cognitive abilities. I have seen older adults have similar symptoms because of a urinary tract infection. For us, it was harder to identify Grandmom's transition from her usual behaviors to behaviors associated with Dementia because some of the traits were so similar.

I have frequently had people ask how we didn't see certain things. Honestly, it's because she didn't change as much to the immediate family as she did to outsiders. People outside of the immediate family got to see the anger, aggression, and cruel streak she had always kept hidden. We didn't know she was suddenly treating people like she had always treated us. As much as people criticized us for not knowing, I judged them right back. The people quickest to have snide comments were the ones that had noticed changes but didn't share those concerns. Then they made hateful comments to alleviate their guilt over keeping quiet.

I also recognize that we all enabled Grandmom to be the person she was by giving in, not questioning her, and accepting her behaviors, probably more than was healthy. On some level, it is a typical parent-child relationship and grandparent-grandchild relationship. Still, in other ways, it was a circus. I now realize that her problems influenced my personality and how I do things. I am regularly learning how her personality and behaviors colored my worldview.

The people we spend the most time with influence who we are for better and worse. I realize now that I never questioned her decisions or actions out loud. It worked best to persuade answers out of her without outright asking. Grandmom seemed to take questions about her choices as a challenge instead of curiosity and often became confrontational. I was a child; how dare I question her? She conditioned me not to ask. But that didn't stop my curiosity, so I learned to maneuver the conversation into getting answers to my questions without asking.

There is almost an inherent need to create reason out of the chaos of Grandmom's emotions, even though I know that is impossible. It is still difficult for me not to feel personally attacked by things she did or said through the years. Her untreated mental health left us all with some concerns of our own. The voice in my head can be pretty critical. I often hear Grandmom's voice when overly critical of myself or others. The things she believed and did, bled over into my actions and thoughts. I am trying to break this cycle. Grandmom battled anxiety and depression all of her adult life, with the last few years becoming exponentially worse. As more people, places, and things became unfamiliar, how could it not exacerbate these feelings. However, the pre-existing mental health concerns were not responsible for every characteristic and behavior displayed while battling Dementia. The depression and anxiety contributed to her Dementia battle just as they contributed to her life.

Getting to Know Grandmom

Born in 1932, like many children born during the great depression; Grandmom had a difficult childhood. The habits, practices, and beliefs developed during her young years would impact her view of the world for the rest of her life. But for her, there was more than just being a child of the depression era.

In 1947, when my grandparents were dating, they were in a car wreck. Grandmom had snuck off from church to go courting. The story varies some over what happened. She sometimes said she busted the car's front windshield out with her forehead, and at other times, a toolbox in the car hit her in the head. No matter the specifics of the car wreck, the fact remains that she had a significant injury. However, because she seemed fine, it was not treated as a source of concern. That was just not how they practiced medicine in 1947, at least not where my grandparents lived. The doctor came to the house, stitched up the cut on her head and knee, and that was that. There was no follow-up treatment, no brain scans, no X-rays, nothing to see if she had brain damage or a fractured skull. Grandmom was only 15 at the time. If she seemed fine, considering what had happened, she must have been fine.

We would find out years later about the extent of Grandmom's head trauma from this event. Even though we saw evidence of trauma through her actions, it remained physically unidentified until Grandmom was in her 70s. While Grandmom was still living independently, she experienced extreme sodium depletion and almost died. This event led to a hospital stay and severe headaches for nearly two years afterward. The scary thing was the way she explained the severe headache. She kept saying someone had hit her in the head and split her head open. No external injuries were visible to support her story; clearly, no one had hit her in the head. Her MRIs also showed no signs of stroke or aneurism. There was no explanation for why her headache pain was so specific, and she remained convinced her head had been split open. However, it did show an interesting bit of historical information. The doctor asked Mom how old Grandmom had been when she fractured her skull. There was no doubt that she had cracked a portion of her frontal bone. The healing process was not seamless, and the regrowth was visible on the scan. Additionally, as her skull healed, the calcified build-up around the fracture grew into the frontal lobe of Grandmom's brain.

This discovery answered some questions and helped provide answers for things that had happened throughout my life. I think each of the immediate family had wondered about a possible traumatic brain injury at some point. We had all heard the car wreck story. I began questioning this possibility when I took Anatomy and Physiology and Introduction to Psychology. The human frontal lobe continues to develop until people reach their mid-twenties; damage before that milestone can drastically impact personality development. It is linked to impulse control, emotional regulation, empathy, and interpreting others' emotions. When we reached this section in those courses, a lightbulb came on. The biggest clue was her lack of empathy. She often had difficulty expressing compassion for others. She even voiced a dislike for the expectation to demonstrate concern for another's feelings when they wouldn't do it for her.

Perhaps I am grasping at straws for personal closure. I am okay with that because it allows me to find closure and move past some hurtful childhood memories. I could also be completely wrong. The trauma to Grandmom's frontal lobe may not have had that much influence on her personality. Perhaps that was just her personality; maybe she was that mean and did not care if she hurt anyone else. Rationalizing another person's motives or actions is not always a healthy coping tool. However, this line of thinking has allowed me to let go of some bitterness. I am finding peace by allowing myself to believe that some of her over-the-top reactions and disproportionate responses were neither my fault nor hers.

Grandmom and Granddad got married in October 1947. When they married, my grandparents were 15 and 17, and both pretended to be a year older to get away with it. They lived in a one-room shack that had previously been a chicken coop. In August of 1948, their first and only son was born. By that time, Grandmom was all of 16, and Granddad was 18. They were still kids by today's standards.

To my understanding, childbirth in the 1940s was another traumatic event for Grandmom. Given her age and what she went through, I cannot imagine how it wouldn't have been life-changing. The baby was breech, and there were complications as a result. After laboring for hours with her son, the infant boy died during birth. The doctor informed Granddad of the loss. But Grandmom was drugged up and left to sleep. I get it; women in the 1940s were too fragile.

Unlike women of the past, the truth was more than 1940s women could handle. They could deliver children with halfway care but didn't deserve closure. Granddad was allowed to see the baby, but Grandmom never saw her infant son. By the time Grandmom left the hospital, all she had was a picture of him and a grave to visit. It is no wonder she didn't deal well with it.

Mom was born a little over a year and a half later, and a sister followed in ten years. Pregnancy was not easy for Grandmom, and none of her children's births was a happy memory. Childbirth was another area that tended to be taboo for her generation. She seldom spoke about it, but there was sadness and bitterness when she did. During her last pregnancy, she was in labor for days, not hours. When we cleaned out her house, we found a letter she had written after giving birth to my aunt. She wrote of thinking she was going to die and how Jesus appeared to her telling her it was not her time.

Her faith was kind of amazing. Grandmom often wrote out prayers and made sure to write down events she viewed as an answered prayer. She had notebooks filled with scripture and her beliefs surrounding specific passages. No matter how chaotic her mind became, her faith remained strong. We found many other examples where she had written of faith.

In 1961, Grandmom experienced tremendous depression during her third pregnancy. She entered a mental health hospital for about a month and underwent Electroconvulsive Therapy (ECT) to treat depression. That procedure left her with severe anxiety and flashbacks. It also did nothing to help her depression, which became a lifelong battle. I cannot imagine how painful it must have been to experience what she did at that hospital. Only to have people that supposedly care about you pretend it didn't happen later in life.

Comparatively, when Grandmom underwent ECT, it was still a newer treatment. The treatment is still in use today, but it has changed over the years. The process of ECT sends electrical currents through a patient's brain, and the electrical current triggers a seizure. In modern medicine, the patient is under anesthesia when undergoing the treatment. However, just as with any medical procedure, the process history is full of failures and improvements. Things that are now standard were once not even considered. For the early recipients of this treatment, receiving anesthesia was not always part of ECT protocol.

Unfortunately, Grandmom was one of many people to receive this treatment in its historically brutal manner. Years later, she would talk about getting "shock treatments" and how she had been awake during the process. I always imagined movie scenes where the restrained and scared patient fights and screams as the electrodes are attached to their temples. I don't know precisely when anesthesia became a mandatory part of the treatment protocol. Unlike today, in 1961, it seems as if it was not a required part. I am thankful to know that patients are not supposed to be awake for the process in modern medicine; yet remain horrified that Grandmom was awake. I cannot imagine how horrible the experience was for her or how any doctor thought this was acceptable.

Unfortunately, even if the doctor had tried sedating Grandmom for the procedure, she had an atypical response to sedatives. Even in her eighties, sedatives did not affect Grandmom like most people, almost seeming to give her an adrenaline boost. She did not relax and often seemed stronger after being given certain ones. If sedatives did not work on her later in life, I do not imagine they would have worked well or at all, even if the doctor made an effort to try them in 1961.

Grandmom was not a success story. Some people believe Grandmom filled in memory gaps of the procedure with imagination. Saying I am offended by the implication that Grandmom had imagined her trauma isn't even close to accurate. This belief infuriates me! Why does another person get to decide Grandmom's trauma is less relevant because the treatment is no longer so barbaric? I am not qualified to judge another's trauma, but disregarding someone's trauma perpetuates mental health stigmas. Grandmom said she was awake during the process and that memory was traumatic. Opinions about the memory's validity are irrelevant; her trauma was real! The tendency to invalidate another's trauma, beliefs, or feelings is societal, but I try not to perpetuate it.

As Grandmom's processing abilities declined with Dementia, her ability to identify threats versus help decreased as well. Any procedure that required restraining her, even for a short time or for her safety, like an MRI, went catastrophically wrong very fast. For example, Grandmom fell, and the care providers attempted to stabilize her legs in case of a hip injury or broken leg. She assaulted the people trying to help her. In the emergency room, the providers tried to stabilize her limbs for x-rays, she continued to fight. They gave her sedatives to relax her, and it got worse. She was violent, lashing out and trying to hurt anyone in arms or legs reach. Grandmom was terrified. Dementia made instances like this more common as the cognitive decline became worse. I believe she vividly relived past events, and there was no way to save her from those memories.

Throughout my childhood, I frequently heard Grandmom say she needed her "nerve pills." I didn't know what they were at that time, but it was most likely valium. She tended to go back to that prescription. The nerve pills were culturally acceptable for women of her generation, much like wine or mommy juice is now. There will be another culturally acceptable mood enhancement method in a few years. There is nothing wrong with using medication, diet, supplements, or exercise to help enhance your quality of life. However, it isn't healthy for anyone when we fail to identify the problem's underlying reason.

I do not recall Grandmom seeing a psychologist during my childhood. Perhaps it was more common for general practitioners to prescribe continued use medications by this time. I find the idea of a general practitioner prescribing Grandmom's medication without follow-up or therapy concerning. There was an underlying issue if she continually needed nerve pills for decades. How was this never followed- up on and remained overlooked? A prescription without proper supervision isn't treatment, and neither is treating a symptom rather than addressing the problem.

Then one day, she stopped saying anything about her nerve pills. I don't know why; I never asked, and she never mentioned them again. However, sometime after the nerve pills left the picture, she started sipping cough syrup. She said she had a tickle in her throat and couldn't seem to get rid of it. She refused to see a doctor over the tickle in her throat, saying she just needed her cough syrup. Sipping cough syrup doesn't sound like a big deal, but her version of a sip was a swig, at least the recommended dose. She was also sipping the 1980s-90s cough syrup with the addictive ingredients that get you high as a kite when you take too much. Suddenly the swigs were happening way more often than recommended. Then one day, just as quickly as it started, it stopped. She stopped carrying a cough syrup with her and never again mentioned the tickle in her throat.

Grandmom did this over and over. A new supplement or over-the-counter medicine she couldn't live without and had to have it with her at all times. Then after months and sometimes even years, suddenly, it would never be mentioned again. We would only find out much later that the need for and fixation on medicines extended to prescription medication.

In addition to anxiety and depression, Grandmom had battled pain. I never remember her not being in pain. She had severe scoliosis, and her left leg was an inch and a half to two inches shorter than her right. Her doctor could not believe she did not limp; she had been that way for so long she had learned to compensate. Mom always hemmed Grandmom's pants because the leg length was so significantly different. I have a fond memory of shopping with Grandmom. I listened outside of the dressing room as she tried on pants and fussed about cheap manufacturers, criticizing their inability to make pants with legs the same length. As I said, she liked to fuss; it made her happy. As Grandmom aged, the pain related to scoliosis became worse as arthritis developed and her spinal disks deteriorated. Grandmom's attempts at pain management led to increased self-medication and eventually abuse and addiction to prescription medication.

Granddad was diagnosed with cancer in early 1987 and would be gone soon after Christmas the same year. He was given

Morphine and a few other high-powered pain medications in tablet form during that time. Grandmom filled all of those prescriptions and all of the refills. Granddad did not take a lot of pain medication while he remained at home. Once he needed the pain medication to that extent, he was in the hospital and would never leave. Grandmom kept all of the prescribed pain medication and took it herself over the years. We found the last few pills squirreled away in her house after moving her into assisted living. That was 15 years after she had moved from the home she shared with Granddad, and that move happened ten years after he had passed.

After I left home, her doctor began prescribing Percocet, Oxycontin, and at one point even Fentanyl for back pain. When she said one no longer worked, the doctor switched it out for another. Grandmom cycling through high-powered pain medication went on for years. While I was home for a visit, she took one of her doctor-approved medications. Then within an hour, she took another pill. I looked at her prescription bottle to see what she was taking, and I told her the prescription said one every six hours. She corrected me and said one every six hours or as needed. So, she could take it as often as she needed, even if it had only been an hour. There was no chance of convincing her she was wrong and that, "as required," wasn't whenever she wanted. I explained that the intent behind as needed was to wait longer than six hours if she wasn't in pain, but there was no convincing her of that. To Grandmom, I did not know what I was talking about, and by the time I left, she had once again convinced me I was wrong.

The pharmacist was the first to identify a problem when Grandmom took a month's worth of Percocet in a single week and went back for a refill. Grandmom had a fit when they would not and could not refill her prescription. Then she contacted her doctor to call in a new one. Instead, the primary care doctor finally realized the other doctors and interns on staff had each been writing prescriptions without checking her history. Instead of addressing the possible medication addiction, they sent her a letter firing her as a patient.

Withdrawal from prescription medication isn't easy. Even though it is a prescription medication, withdrawal is still withdrawal. But for Grandmom, the idea that it could be an addiction was unheard of and offensive. The doctor would never give her something addictive. She believed that doctors were trusted above anyone else and had the patient's best interest at heart. She was devastated by that letter firing her as a patient. Truthfully, the letter was callous and rude. I read it later and was livid. There was no reason to be that unprofessional and disrespectful. I believe it was an effort to cover their errors and blame her for the problem.

Grandmom was one of many people that became part of the prescription drug epidemic running rampant through the Appalachian region during that time.

Daily visits to control Grandmom's medication became Mom's responsibility. Grandmom resented this and made a point to voice her discontent at every opportunity. Grandmom did not like any implication that she could not take care of herself and required help. It was a daily battle. At that time, I was too far away to visit frequently. Hearing what Mom was going through and listening to her doubts, and beating herself up over not doing enough was when I started advocating for outside help and services. Grandmom wouldn't have liked them any better, but the attacks would not have been as personal. Unfortunately, we would learn, too late to be helpful, that Grandmom was in better spirits and displayed happier behaviors around strangers rather than immediate family.

Don't Forget Your Company Manners

Realistically we should have predicted that Grandmom would at least pretend she liked strangers better than her family. She had always been good at hiding what she was thinking from acquaintances. Grandmom was a believer in using company manners. She was often more critical and demanding with the immediate family.

Everybody has a version of company manners. My family used this term, but other people may say something different. These are the behaviors and expectations that come up in various aspects of life. I have frequently heard others say use your indoor voice, school behaviors, and business etiquette throughout my life. The helpful and encouraging phrases everyone I know has said at some point. As an adult, company manners provide detachment, keeping adults on good terms with one another. In-depth discussions are limited until people know each other better or have more firmly established the image we want others to see and believe. I think it is a throw-back idea revolving around making an excellent first impression and attempting to be the best-liked version of ourselves. Not necessarily the best version of ourselves, but the version we believe best for a specific situation. There is nothing wrong with this; it is perfectly normal and often necessary behavior. Imagine the chaos if we didn't do this sometimes. Company manners encompassed these ideas and covered any behavior used more with people we don't know.

When we were expecting visitors outside of the immediate family or close friends, Mom said to use our company manners. She said this, hoping we would not act like wild animals while people visited. Sometimes this worked, but sometimes there were too many opportunities for us to get into trouble. It would be fun trouble but trouble all the same. I am guilty of telling my nieces and nephews to use their company manners. It is my default method of encouragement to be on their best behavior.

Grandmom was skilled with company manners. In Grandmom's case, company manners were the personality traits and characteristics displayed when anyone outside of the immediate family was present. She put on company manners when anyone other than Granddad, Mom, me, my brother, or Aunt were around. These characteristics are the way most people remember her. She was fun and funny, with a wicked sense of humor, loved practical jokes, and had a generous heart. Again, for Grandmom, how she thought others saw her was always extremely important. However, she had a different personality and acted differently with the immediate family. She was harsh, judgmental, and critical. She often used things she had done for you, even imagined ones, as a manipulation strategy. When she treated someone poorly, she always had a justification for her actions that painted her in the best light. Her explanations often revolved around what she believed she had done for them, especially with close family.

These behaviors are generally more toned-down versions of who we are. For Grandmom, these behaviors were more like an alter ego. The changing behaviors contribute to why our perceptions of other people often vary. People have different experiences and memories with the same person. When Grandmom believed no one was around to think poorly of her, she was very different. It was exhausting. I never understood how someone could keep up an image for extended periods. How do people pretend to be someone they aren't, day in and day out, without ever actually being that person? Eventually, the unpolished version of me gets out no matter how well I try to hide.

Additionally, Grandmom often treated

people differently to their faces than she did behind their backs. Perhaps this is a generational difference. I may be polite to someone I don't like, but I certainly don't hang out with them, then complain about not wanting to be around them.
Grandmom did this with everyone. I have never been able to tell if she really disliked everyone, just liked complaining, or something else was going on entirely. It was so confusing. But at the same time, I knew she fussed about me as soon as I was out of sight. She would talk about all of us, and the stories she would tell fluctuated between hurtful and hilarious. The difference between how Grandmom acted and what she said contributed to drastically different perceptions of her.

    I used to wonder if she liked others that much more than us? Perhaps as a family, we were just the worst. As an adult, I realize that even if she disliked us to that extent, she disliked everyone else as well. She was generally unhappy throughout my lifetime. It has taken a long time to realize her unhappiness wasn't on me or anyone else to fix. Even though we tried to keep her happy, this was a conditioned response. She expected us to make her happy and saw her happiness as our responsibility. We would never be enough to make her happy because she didn't know what she needed to be satisfied. To this day, I have no idea what would have helped her find happiness. It is a mystery that I will never know the answer to, and I am okay with leaving it unanswered.

Part of Grandmom's image was her generosity and good heart. These were both true; she was often very generous and sometimes extraordinarily kind. But the opposite was also true. When Grandmom did something for you, you owed her, and there was never a satisfactory return. She gave nothing without strings attached. Grandmom frequently grumbled about ungrateful relatives. She often dwelled on something she had given or done for another and her unjust treatment in return.

The more events Grandmom forgot, the wilder the complaints became. Events from 20 years before became fresh new complaints, with forgotten or incorrect details. Things she thought she had done were often inaccurate. Grandmom began filling in parts from her imagination or attributing deeds to random people. There was a time she told anyone that would listen about buying me a house and a car, saying what a terrible person I was for running off across the country afterward. It was interesting because she did this with me, standing right there, and she hadn't bought me a house or a car. I got used to the dirty looks people gave me.

Generally, something would distract her after a bit, and she would move on. After the first attempt to correct her misconception, I gave up and just let people think the worst. During the rant, there was no stopping her; she believed what she was saying and attempting to correct her belief made her angry.

The strange thing about this specific rant is that I don't even know if she had purchased a car or house for someone else. That isn't something she would have mentioned in casual conversation. The only reason she would have talked about it with me was to complain that she had done it for someone that was not appropriately grateful. It is entirely possible that she made a purchase like this at some point years prior or co-signed a loan for a significant amount for someone and then couldn't remember who. In some flawed form of rationalization, she defaulted to me in the memory. After all, I was her granddaughter, and that seems logical. Therefore, it must have been me because why would she do something like that for anyone else?

Having no understanding of why Grandmom behaved in specific ways left young me hurt and sad more often than not. It took outside influences and interacting with different people to help me move past the childhood hurt. Many behaviors were about her and had nothing to do with me, even though those actions impacted me. But that was a complex concept to grasp as a child.

I believe it is standard to question why someone else treats you one way or another, especially when that person is a loved one. But I find it unhealthy long term to dwell on the why. Sometimes they are just that way. Understanding what drives another's personality can become an exhausting rabbit hole. Finding reason becomes a time-consuming hamster wheel with zero answers when the loved one doesn't fully understand their actions.

I have learned to accept, I will never fully know who Grandmom was, and I will also never know how she truly felt about any of us. Her ability to switch from loving and fun to critical and cruel happened often and fast. It is a bizarre feeling to care for someone who seems to love and hate you simultaneously. Her emotions dictated how she reacted to everyone around her, and we were often just along for the ride. I wondered if she wasn't a narcissist at times because her world revolved around her. As I have gotten older, I realize most of her actions were not deliberate. She did not deliberately gaslight or withhold affection for a specific effect. She just did these things without planning. She was more like dealing with a moody and dramatic teenager, almost like her personality development had been stunted.

Grandmom's a Vampire

Grandmom could be so much fun when she had a good day. But if she had a bad one, she could suck the life out of you within a few minutes. It was draining to be around her when she had a bad day or if you made her mad. On good days, she was the life of the party, laughing and joking. She was an absolute joy to be around on those days. But her mood dictated how everyone around her had to act.

I learned very early in life how to assess her moods and potential reactions. The need to react accordingly around her contributed to how I learned to observe other people's emotions and respond accordingly. As an adult, I am aware this level of hyper-vigilance is emotionally draining and generally annoying. For me, constant awareness and a need to respond to others' emotions have left me a nervous wreck. I hate it. It leads to fake empathy and wears me out. Somehow, I never learned to prevent her bad mood, irritation, or depression from putting me in the same state. It took me years to realize it is acceptable to walk away from someone having that effect on me. But even then, I couldn't do that with her.

Grandmom seemed like the complete

opposite to my Granddad. When I was young, I thought the phrase opposites attract fit them perfectly. He loved to laugh and was generally fun; he enjoyed life. He passed away two days after Christmas, not long after his 57th birthday. His passing led to one of Grandmom's more predictable emotions.

I had already given Granddad his Christmas present the year that he died. Then with his death, funeral, and just not being in the spirit, we didn't get around to opening presents until much later. Grandmom decided that I should have the present I had given Granddad back. I don't remember what I got that year. I only remember his gift from me was wrapped up and returned to me inside one of my presents. As you can imagine, I am not too fond of Christmas. I honestly have no clue what she was thinking. But I still have that coffee cup. I have been carrying it around every move for over 30 years. I don't want it, it makes me cry, and I am incapable of getting rid of it. How messed up is that?

For the next 29 years, December was a month of depression. If we visited her in a joyous mood, Grandmom would make sure it went away. She became almost angry if we were not appropriately sad. It was tough for me to mope for an entire month. Don't get me wrong, I missed

Granddad, and I still miss him. But I don't think he would have wanted any of us to wallow in misery year after year.

I was not a depressed kid, and this was very draining year after year. However, I spent 29 years allowing Grandmom to dictate that December was a month of sadness, and it made me miserable. That is not my natural state; endless sadness exhausts me, just like infinite perkiness does. I like balance. I still have issues with Christmas. But I am trying. I learned a lot about what not to do during a holiday. The year she died, I went all out on the holidays and continue every year since. I make an effort to fill others with joy in the season. I don't want to be why anyone cries during the holiday, especially kids. It can be challenging and easy to fall back into the routine, but I refuse to be a Christmas joy thief.

Even with the depression and moodiness, Grandmom was a very typical Grandparent in many ways. She took on many roles and was an active participant in my childhood and young adult life. I believe, like many grandparents, she preferred her grandkids to her kids. After all, when grandkids decide to act like evil little monsters, they can go home! It is the same with having nieces and nephews; we get the fun without the constant responsibility. As a grandchild, I got away with a lot more. But was not wholly free from her wrath on occasion. Does wrath sound dramatic? Perhaps bullying behavior is more appropriate.

For instance, I fear escalators and learned, later in life, that poor vision contributed significantly to that fear. Escalators with the painted stair edge help, but the fear remains, and it still takes me a bit to get on. When I was about 13, Grandmom and I were in a mall. She thought I was deliberately trying to embarrass her by not getting on the escalator as quickly as she determined I should. She growled that people were looking at us, grabbed my wrist, dug in her nails, and jerked. I fell headfirst down the escalator.

People were indeed looking at us then. After regaining my footing, I was shocked and ready for a fight. I think Grandmom recognized this, and her demeanor changed. She treated it like it had all been a practical joke. Oh, how funny I was trying to scare her and throwing myself down the escalator. Grandmom did not ask if I was okay, say sorry, or even acknowledge doing anything wrong. I still cannot simply step onto an escalator; I have to give myself a pep talk over 30 years later. And I also understand that in present times, that action bordered on child abuse. It wasn't an accident, and there was a real possibility of serious injury. But I wasn't, and it happened in the late 80s early 90s, so even though people looked, it wasn't the same.

For the most part, Grandmom was a very typical woman of her generation. She wasn't an evil person nor a saint. Like the rest of us, she had many flaws and eccentricities. Her impulse control and thought processes were always slightly off compared to what society views as typical. Sometimes her actions were hurtful because she didn't think them through. At others, the behaviors were cruel because she intended them to be. It was the same as when she was being kind.

Our family became victims of an imperfect mental health system. Once medication stopped being an option, she stopped seeing her therapist. After the ECT, there were no efforts to help her outside of pills, and she didn't have the skills to help herself. As an adult, I recognize the misfortune of the situation, and I am no longer mad at her for the way she was. However, I also realize that some of my personality quirks developed from dealing with and responding to her issues.

Dementia, not Alzheimer's

I developed concerns about brain health after Grandmom's diagnosis; seeing what Dementia did to her frightened me. When I am scared, I spiral, catastrophizing at a horrific level. If there is a worst-case scenario, I can imagine it in great detail. I experienced panic every time I forgot to complete parts of my to-do list or failed to get everything from the store. I cannot help but think everyone goes through this as we watch our loved ones change.

I control some of my catastrophizing through learning. I believe information is power. I was relieved that needing a store list or physical to-do list for memory cues is normal brain aging. However, an inability to remember how to complete steps in a daily activity from my to-do list would be abnormal. I was even relieved that beginning to forget the names of everyday objects later in life is also considered typical declining brain function.

Like our bodies, our brains begin to decline as soon as they reach peak development, and it is typical for brains to shrink as we age. However, it was disheartening to learn that the shrinking begins to happen a lot earlier than I would have liked to believe. I expected reading glasses near 40 but learning that brain shrinkage had been occurring long before that freaked me out. So I set out to learn about typical versus atypical aging. I soon realized that there was so much I could never possibly know all of it.

The article "Normal Cognitive Aging" addresses typical age-related degeneration that happens gradually with memory, conceptual reasoning, and how fast we process information or carry out actions (Harada et al., 2013). I found the article helpful in calming an out-of-control spiral when I convinced myself I was turning into Grandmom. So it is normal to have more trouble understanding new abstract ideas or for the understanding to come slower. Yet, it is abnormal to forget the order we get dressed. For example, undergarments go under clothing, and coats go on over the clothing; any reversing of this would cause concern. Routines and steps to complete daily activities should stay with us longer. A normally aging brain should allow the individual to continue completing daily activities independently within physical limitations, taking medication, and showering. (Harada et al., 2013)

Dementia is the broadest term for cognitive decline, and Alzheimer's is the largest category of Dementia. The

Alzheimer's Association defines Dementia as a general category of conditions related to abnormal brain changes. (alz.org) While some cognitive decline is considered a normal part of aging, Dementia is not a typical part of aging. It is an outdated and harmful stereotype to assume everyone loses their minds when older. This stereotype facilitates elder abuse and allows for declining care standards because "they don't know what they are talking about."

There are numerous reasons why cognitive impairments may develop in a person. Different events or actions can facilitate the development of Dementia, including accidents or head traumas, and drug or alcohol abuse. In Grandmom's situation, there was a history of head trauma, depression, and prescription drug abuse. I am honestly no longer surprised that she experienced abnormal cognition decline as she aged. Her brain had gotten a severe workout during her lifetime.

Grandmom had Dementia, even though it got called Alzheimer's frequently. Alzheimer's and Dementia are the same and not the same. The two terms often get used interchangeably, but we should make an effort to identify each disease correctly as it applies to individual people. Each individual's decline and treatment plans will differ between the diagnoses.

Having a better understanding of the specific form of Dementia as early as possible gives the person the best potential for treatment. Grandmom did not develop the physical symptoms associated with Alzheimer's. Her body stayed strong until the very end; it was her mind that failed. Her doctor was impressed at how physically healthy she was when she first moved into assisted living. Grandmom was exceptionally physically healthy for her age. The doctor commented that she could potentially live another twenty years.

Because Alzheimer's disease is the largest category under Dementia, it became the default when others learned of Grandmom's changing health. The different diseases under the Dementia heading have overlapping similarities and unique characteristics related to that specific diagnosis. So it is entirely understandable why this happens. The broadest symptom of Dementia is memory problems. Memory problems may include not remembering new information or not recalling the steps in an activity performed frequently. However, some of the differences in the actual diagnosis led to misunderstandings about what we should or should not do, mostly from people not on the care team.

Grandmom was meticulous with note-taking and reminders; this habit increased as she recognized she was becoming more forgetful. According to the Alzheimer's Association, Alzheimer's is a progressive disease that starts mild and worsens; changes may be more noticeable to family and friends first. (alz.org) We did not notice first. Grandmom denied having any problems, but we later found letters she wrote to herself describing her experiences.

Additionally, Alzheimer's impacts the body. The person has problems walking and moving around, talking becomes more challenging, and conversation becomes less frequent. These characteristics may seem mild at first but get worse over time. Grandmom's physical limitations were not a result of cognitive decline. However, scoliosis and osteoarthritis became more painful and limiting, as expected.

The vast difference in physical and mental health led to some problems with her overall care. Grandmom didn't always remember she was sick or injured. We were very blessed that her caregivers stayed vigilant. One of the most complex parts is finding the balance among the care providers, family members, and doctors of what is medically necessary at this point. What areas will improve Grandmom's life versus what will decrease her quality of life?

Her doctor still felt she needed to keep up with standard health screenings. Again, this is usually a good thing for a doctor to encourage. However, some of these health screens required preparation or were uncomfortable. The doctor wanted Grandmom to have a mammogram done as part of a routine cancer screening for a physical. Also, ordinarily, a good and perfectly acceptable test to want. She didn't want to have a mammogram when she knew why she needed one. But when she didn't remember why she needed to do the things, it made them an even more challenging process to get through.

These types of tests and screening had a way of placing us in a no-win situation every time. If we don't do it, we don't care about her health. If we have the tests and it shows something serious, we don't care about her quality of life. There was a lot of guilt to go around when making these decisions. The decision to test or not to test is another area where people will judge the decisions no matter what the care team decides is best. There will always be someone around to say how the choice was wrong. After the fact, it is easy to say ignore those people, but it was much harder advice to live by when it was happening. And I was a little mean when people began to question Mom's and Auntie's decisions, like make the busybodies cry mean. I don't recommend that, but it does work.

When it came to Grandmom's doctor, it wasn't judgment but legitimate care for her wellbeing that made them pushy. It was easy to forget her level of cognitive decline when you did not see her every day. Besides, Grandmom was very good at making you believe that she was entirely in control, so I don't blame the doctors for forgetting this initially. One of the more helpful ways to reach the least objectionable decision is by asking a specific question. It is a sneaky yet straightforward question that almost always makes the doctor mad, at least at first. If the outcome is life-threatening, what next?

While the doctor was initially insistent that she have the mammogram because she might have breast cancer. We could not see any benefit because she would not undergo treatment. How do you explain chemo, radiation, or removal surgeries to someone who doesn't remember having cancer? After a family discussion, we opted to decline the test. Even the doctor had to accept that it is hard to justify painful interventions or treatments that deteriorate life quality to someone with severe Dementia.

Upon further discussion, the care team agreed that even a positive cancer diagnosis would not decrease her quality of life. Given her age and level of cognitive decline, treatment would not improve her life. I kept arguing for quality over quantity. I pushed for her remaining life to be as enjoyable as possible and do nothing that would hinder each day. It may sound cruel that I advocated not to extend her life by any means necessary. But I find the extension of life at the expense of quality a much more heartless action.

Quirks and Clues

Grandmom impressively masked her Dementia for years. Only looking back, personality changes and increases in specific characteristics begin making sense. Grandmom always had a few habitual actions. It wasn't uncommon for her to be suspicious and slightly paranoid regarding her money. Dementia signs and symptoms sometimes include these behaviors. However, they are not reliable signs when someone is that way already.

Looking back, identifying when the behaviors became worse becomes easier. Yet, it was harder to see the behaviors as a sign while it was happening. As Dementia progressed, so did the habitual actions, suspicion, and paranoia. After the fact, the change is noticeable but not the best clue in that given moment. I have to remind myself of that fact regularly because there are still times when I think we could have done better or ask myself how we didn't see things that are now so clear.

Grandmom had always kept detailed notes and records. I realize now it was a form of journaling, just not what I typically think of as a journal. There wasn't a dedicated book to keep her thoughts. Instead, it was letters or notes on a postcard. She often kept information about events on pictures. Grandmom recorded our family history on the back of photographs. The photo backs usually contained people's full names, the date, and the event. It is a habit I picked up pre-digital age, and it is still helpful.

After she passed, going through her photo albums was an epic photo history of our family. But we could see her Dementia progression on the backs of photos too. As she began to forget people, she wrote their relationship to the others in the picture. Often including vague references to how she knew them or where the event took place. She marked through the information on some photos and replaced it with their name or more detailed information. I assume she remembered at a later time who they were. Her handwriting changed as well and became less uniform. Not that Grandmom's writing had always been neat, but it was more structurally consistent. The lines on paper did not mean as much, and the letters were sporadic in height or width. For me, this is normal handwriting because I have always been a bit of a messy writer. However, for Grandmom, it was an indicator of her changing mind.

Grandmom loved cookbooks and recipes, but she did not like to cook. I can't blame her. At least, I know where I came by this trait. She could cook well enough to survive, but she wasn't a great cook. She had tons of printed cookbooks and then had loads of adhesive page photo albums filled with recipes she had snipped from magazines, boxes, and things. She also kept notes on the recipes and in the cookbooks. She would write down what event or where she took the dish whenever she made something. When she received a recipe from someone, she wrote who had given it to her, where they were, and any other details she deemed necessary. I think this was another way she journaled and kept track of events. Grandmom had kept notes like this for so long that there is no way to know when she started forgetting things versus a simple habit.

As Grandmom got older, she continued to collect recipes. But knowing that she wasn't going to fix any of them, she began creating a homemade cookbook for me and filled it with recipes. Grandmom did this knowing that I am also not a cook. For me, even cooking to survive is questionable, and my entire family knows this. Grandmom avoided cooking whenever possible, but for some reason, she seemed to think it was unacceptable that I also disdained cooking.

To this day, I am baffled by her thinking. And in this situation, it was not something she forgot I could or couldn't do. As long as Grandmom remembered me, she knew I couldn't cook and thought she could wish me or shame me into getting better at it with loads of recipes. There were notes throughout the cookbook about my inability to cook and my determination not to learn. I laughed so hard when we found the cookbook. She would be a little disappointed her plan didn't work. I still can't cook, and my sister has the cookbook. After all, someone needed to use it; it has some good recipes.

Grandmom also kept many notes, references, and other information in Bibles, and she had a lot of them. We found a load of Bibles in all shapes and sizes, decorative and plain. Keeping a family history in the Bible with a record of births, deaths, and marriages is a common practice for my family on all sides. If you needed to know a birthday, the coffee table Bible was the first place to look. Grandmom kept notes on her desires after her death, her funeral, and other things like that in her Bibles. She kept notes about scripture and what they meant to her in the margins. Again, all pretty standard practices, just the quantity of Bibles, made it a remarkable find.

There were also a large number of the Bibles designated as my aunt's property.

Not a single Bible but a LOT of Bibles, in all sizes. It felt like Grandmom had stashed at least one Bible in every room in the house for Auntie, and each one had a dedication in the front cover to her. If you have ever felt judged by a Christian, imagine going through their house and finding Bible after Bible designated as your property. Each new Bible brought laughter to a rather sad event. Going through another person's possessions is never easy, no matter the reason, but Grandmom kept us on our toes. I still want to know what Auntie had done for Grandmom to decide she needed all those Bibles?

This situation may have been because Grandmom did have a generous side and would purchase gifts she thought someone needed. I imagine in the case where she had multiple similar items for someone she had forgotten about already buying it. For Auntie, it was Bibles; for me, it was clothing irons and hand mixers. After I moved away from home, Grandmom decided I needed household items. She wasn't wrong; I did need some things, but what she decided I needed became a curious mix.

One of the well-known box stores used to have a specific clothing iron and hand mixer brand that only cost $5. It was a great deal, and they worked well enough.

The thing is, Grandmom kept buying me those two items repeatedly. She would see them, decide I needed them, and I was the proud owner of a new set. I told Grandmom I already had those items and that she was the one who bought them for me. Grandmom said it didn't matter I should keep them; they were inexpensive and probably wouldn't last too long. I thought she might be right, so I did. Eventually, I had three of each at my place, she had given Mom a couple more for me, and we found more when we went through her closets. I realize now that this was probably an early indicator of forgetfulness. But honestly, at the time, her argument made sense. They lasted longer than any of us predicted. As one died, I opened another. I still have one iron in a box, never been opened; I haven't needed to iron anything in recent years. And that one remaining iron makes me smile.

Grandmom also decided I needed to take some of her extra kitchen dishes instead of buying any. She had multiple sets; there were so many place settings from when she used to host large family events like birthdays, Thanksgiving, and Christmas. She had stopped hosting the events several years before and felt like she could get rid of some items; it seemed like a good plan.

She sent a box of items home with me, and once home, I opened them to see which set she gave me. I was so confused when emptying that box; I had three plates, bowls, cups, spoons, forks, and knives. Three, why three? Don't get me wrong, I was thankful for dishes not made from plastic, but the odd number threw me. There were multiple sets of two and four, so what was up with three? The next time I saw Grandmom, I had to ask, why three? Her answer was logic at its finest. She still needed one!

Grandmom had been getting rid of sets of dishes. Later, I learned she sent most of them to Mom's house with the expectation that Mom needed them to host the family events from now on. So when Grandmom decided I had to have dishes, there was only one set of four left, and she kept one of each item for herself.

I ask why not keep the set of four for herself? She raised her eyebrows at me, scoffed, and said she didn't need four; she only needed one. If she had more dishes, people would expect her to fix them something to eat. Grandmom was beginning not to care how others saw her. Even this seemingly small thing was an early indicator of losing interest in others' perceptions of her. Hosting family events had been an important area of her life. I don't believe she liked to host these events, at least not to the scale she had done, but others expected her to host. People bragged on her and complimented her, so she did this out of a perception of duty. So she got rid of the ability to host, no dishes, no problem.

Grandmom had lots of things, partly because she had collections of multiples. However, she also tended to collect stuff in sets of four. There were lots of odd collections. She had amassed four sets of blue and white patterned china dishes, Desert Storm and Desert Shield items, and State Quarter sets, to name a few. She told me once the reason behind her collecting in fours, one set for me, my brother, Mom, and Auntie. It was a deliberate action on her part and was a part of who she had always been. Grandmom thought each of these collections might someday be valuable; if we had them, we could sell them. But we were not supposed to use them, especially the blue china dishes. Again they were to be kept and sold if we needed money.

The little quirks and eccentricities became increasingly visible as Grandmom struggled to mask her Dementia symptoms. But this is another area where I work to remind myself it is only apparent afterward. At the time, it was just another quirk. Sometimes she asked Mom to make a phone call for her or return something to a store, but that was the end of helping her. Grandmom was exceedingly independent. If Grandmom thought it would be unpleasant, she had Mom do it instead. But that wasn't a new trait. It was something she had always done.

We have all questioned if we should have intervened sooner. Looking back over the events as a whole instead of moments, I can quickly identify areas for change. But that is the beauty of reflection; we beat ourselves up over things we could not possibly have known at the moment. After Grandmom took a month's worth of medication in one week, she required more help. However, Grandmom did not view this as help but rather an attempt to control her. It was an unpleasant experience for everyone. Grandmom was living independently, in her own home, with limited assistance for the most part. And when asked, that is what she wanted to continue doing. But that is not what she had always said nor what she had written out as instructions to us.

The move into assisted living was ushered in by a car wreck. Grandmom loved to go out for a drive. It would have broken her heart to take away her last semblance of freedom, but Grandmom's final car wreck brought on significant changes in cognitive function within just a few days. Until that point, Grandmom would seem to have a cognitive decline in a specific area of her life and then plateau for an extended period. It appears that the progression and plateaus cycle contributed to Grandmom's ability to continue functioning independently for longer, with her detailed note system helping disguise her decline.

The inevitable question that people love to ask is, "why did she still have a driver's license," or the other favorite, "why did she have a car?" Well, if it isn't clear by now, we made mistakes, and I don't know anyone that has gone through an experience like this that comes out the other side feeling like they did everything right. From the time Granddad died, Grandmom accused Mom of trying to take her independence, and she told everyone how we plotted against her. Grandmom used that accusation as a weapon, and because of this, Mom went to extremes to allow Grandmom complete autonomy. Still, whenever Grandmom didn't get her way, the accusation came out, and it began long before there was even a hint of cognitive decline.

Grandmom had a license and a car because we had no proof that she was unsafe with either of these things. The decision seems easy after the fact. But at the time, even the suggestion to not drive or drive less resulted in an epic fight. Her sisters would come over to spend the day, they would get into the car with her driving, and none mentioned any concerns about her driving skills. Not once did they voice any need for worry, or a least they would not admit to ever being concerned about her driving. And even if they had expressed concerns, poor driving skills aren't always an indicator of cognitive decline.

There is also the possibility that Grandmom would have done what she wanted and drove anyway. She totaled the car in her last accident, and even then, she tried to get a new one. She was adamant that she was an excellent driver, and the only thing that kept her from it after the wreck was the totaled car. At the accident, the cop on the scene told my step-dad that someone should probably take her license away "this time." Step-dad asked the cop, "what do you mean this time?" Remember, the people that rode with her most often never voiced concern. Come to find out, Grandmom was a bit of a menace on the road, and the cops were well aware she probably shouldn't drive, but they also didn't want to take her license away.

The process of taking an adult family member's driver's license away is a little more complicated than it appears. There is some hesitance on multiple levels to take a senior citizen's license because it can quickly become an age discrimination concern. The rules and laws are often complex and inconsistent. Even getting the doctor to support a recommendation for taking her license away didn't happen until that wreck. Until there was an event, in this case, the car wreck, that demonstrated enough proof that she was unsafe behind the wheel, no one would intervene. Minor traffic incidents don't count as proof. We were the only ones responsible for making the decision, and the outside agencies that made suggestions did not back us at any point. Even initially after the wreck, there was hesitance. Then she began a rapid and noticeable decline. Suddenly, we were all not imagining things.

Conversations with Dead Relatives

Grandmom always switched up our names. She would be talking to me and confuse my name with her daughters' names my whole life. I look so much like the two of them that it is easy to see how she interchanged our names. But to be fair, Grandmom even mixed in my brother's name on occasion. The name swapping was never a big deal. If she wanted my attention, she called me by everyone else's name, even the dog's name, before calling mine. I have a large extended family with dozens of cousins, aunts, and uncles. It is clear that we are all related, we all favor, so mixing up names isn't a big deal.

Name swapping is a normal thing for everyone in our family. However, while running down the list of family members, switching out names, until finding the correct one, Grandmom still had some consistency. Every person she called me was a living relative. Grandmom never called me by any of the deceased relatives' names. The name swapping did not become a clue into her declining cognitive state until the dead relatives got involved. She was not talking to herself or swapping a name for a deceased relative. She started thinking I was the deceased person and was talking to them at that moment. The less Grandmom recognized me as her adult Granddaughter, the more she confused me with Mom and Auntie and her sisters and sisters-in-law.

I first told Mom, Grandmom needed help while home for a visit. I had been gone for an extended time, and Grandmom didn't recognize me upon seeing me. I assumed it was my changing hair color or style, a weight gain or loss, and many things that could make my appearance different. I was not concerned that she didn't know me on sight. However, after I introduced myself, she asked Toni who? I said, Toni, your granddaughter? I honestly confused myself for a moment. She had a knack for making me think I was the one that had forgotten something. She laughed and said something about my hair being different. She went on to ask how I expected people to recognize me when I changed it all the time. We didn't discuss why she didn't know me by my name.

We visited and talked. Grandmom told me the same story several times; that happened a lot, yet it wasn't concerning. She called me by other family members' names; again, no cause for concern. However, when she chewed me out over something Auntie was doing, I began to see there might be a problem. At first, I tried correcting her.

Grandmom, I'm Toni.

Grandmom, I don't live in Arizona

I lived in Tennessee and was not doing whatever *shameful thing* Auntie was supposedly doing. Grandmom did not appreciate me blaming someone else, and I needed to own up to what I was doing. Have I mentioned Grandmom was a little dramatic? She was highly offended by my actions, and I would allow her to say her peace. So I took the butt chewing, and I have not let Auntie live that down.

The angry, confused lecture concerned me. Not because Grandmom fussed at me; she did that a lot. However, this was the first time she thought I was someone else and was adamant about that belief to the point of anger. At that point, the angry outburst seemed to alter reality for her on some level. She was sure I was my aunt.

After Grandmom finished lecturing Auntie, we continued talking; as quickly as the lecture started, she was done like it never happened. However, our conversation changed; she seemed drained and more confused. Now the family members she confused me for expanded to great aunts, including two who had passed away many years before. This change was another first. Grandmom had never called me by either of those great Aunts' names. Grandmom swapping out our names was typical, but person swapping was new. Grandmom's conversations with dead relatives would become more common as Dementia progressed. She insisted that she knew who you were even if you didn't.

I became used to being called my great aunts' names and learned quickly not to correct whatever name she called me. Something as seemingly simple as name correction soon became a significant source of anxiety. Grandmom was no longer name swapping because we all look alike. She often had a full-on person swap moment. These were tricky because Grandmom discussed past events or memories. Often expecting the person she was talking with to fill in forgotten details. When it was a story I knew, I went along with it, filling in more information or coaching Grandmom through whatever she was remembering. However, sometimes she brought up things only the other participants knew. When this happened, I would redirect her or tell her I didn't remember the details because my memory had gotten fuzzy too.

I often ask myself if going along with her during these events was the best way to approach the situation. It becomes the ethical question for caregiving and cognitive decline. The truth is there isn't a correct answer, just a best for your loved one answer. When memory care is the goal, I recommend seeking professional guidance with the loved one's care team. The professionals know how to best address this and offer family support in this area. Professional services may allow for great strides with memory preservation, depending on the individual's needs. However, it isn't a stress-free endeavor and depends on the individual's situation and needs. Expecting every interaction with the family to be a memory care therapy session is impractical.

Friends and other family members quickly judged how we dealt with Grandmom. They all had input but never offered solutions. Here's the thing, I believe in doing the best you can with what you have and leaving the professional therapies to professionals whenever possible. Professionals generally do not take it personally when called the wrong name or reintroduce themselves at every meeting. It is sad and hurtful to watch family members continually reintroducing themselves. But it has to happen, and that process of continual reintroduction is a challenging adjustment for family's members. Reminding a loved one who you are is one of those unpleasant gut-check moments, a glaring cue that they are slipping further away. I felt like I was losing my history as she forgot me. It hurts, feels personal, and is hard to remember that it isn't. Grandmom didn't choose to forget me or anyone else but knowing that didn't make it hurt any less.

Being Forgotten

I felt I had prepared myself with knowledge and knew that Grandmom might not remember people. However, I wasn't as prepared as I thought to be one of the people she forgot. Information on Dementia and the path of forgetfulness is widely available in accredited scientific reporting and anecdotal evidence. As we grow, we change, so I expect my distant relatives or even friends' elderly relatives not to remember me. Now that I am older, it is easier to see how we are less recognizable after extended absences. However, there is a difference between being unrecognized and being forgotten.

Several years before Grandmom began to display signs of Dementia, my friend's grandfather had fought his own battle. Much like Grandmom, he was more stubborn and creative about the disease, keeping the family on their toes with his antics. He was the first experience I had with someone leaving the room, returning within a few minutes, only to ask who I was and how I got into his house. Even knowing that was possible, I was in no way emotionally prepared for Grandmom to forget me. It isn't the same when it is someone you have been close with all of your life. For me, it was the emotional equivalent of a falling dream; only reality didn't change after waking. As much as this hurt, I chose to see the fascinating insight that this new reality offered.

One of my last visits with Grandmom is one of the more beautiful aspects of being forgotten. I stopped by her room in the assisted living facility, introduced myself, and asked if she wanted company. When Grandmom heard my name, she responded with some excitement, "Oh, that is my Granddaughter's name." I told her that was wonderful and spoke of it being a grand coincidence because it wasn't a common name. I was holding out hope that she would recognize me. She then told me all about myself or the version of me she remembered.

I was cute and sweet.

    Oh, how I could make her laugh.

        I was such a little performer.

        I was also three.

I knew in those moments that she might never again know who the woman in front of her was. She no longer had any recollection of the adult version of me. Being forgotten entirely by a loved one is shocking and heartbreaking. I felt a mixture of sadness, anger, and confusion all in those few seconds. However, I chose not to focus on that or force her to try and see me. Instead, intently I listened to her as she told me all about myself and how she thought the world of her little granddaughter.

Knowing Grandmom thought the world of her little granddaughter but had forgotten me at the same time was hard to accept. It is frightening that a person's mind can turn against them to such a degree. That was one of my last visits with her. I stopped visiting about a year before she passed. Seeing me began to create stress for her. The strong family resemblance was more than Grandmom could process. I looked too much like someone she felt she should know but couldn't place, which made her anxious. I could no longer improve the quality of her life with those visits.

On several occasions, well-meaning jerks have informed me that I should have tried anyway and just left if I upset her. People that do not have any horse in the race will always have comments. I made my choices, whether right or wrong. I chose not to see her. I decided not to disrupt her life and leave behind a mess. Because once I left, someone else ended up being responsible for calming her. People who believe you should try anyway regardless of the pain and stress caused to the loved one also tend to remain oblivious to the chaos left in their wake. The stress and disruption extended far beyond Grandmom and a single stressful visitor.

The turmoil often spread to other residents in the assisted living facility.

Grandmom was combative, and her agitation extended to other residents and the staff members. Her behavior had an impact on other people and their quality of life. Knowing that we were triggering her unhappiness is a hard truth to accept. The care team kept logs of visits and how she responded to them. The record speaks for itself, and seeing immediate family upset her for whatever reason. We had to accept that sometimes her quality of life was better without interacting with us. There was a lot of judgment because of limiting in-person visits. According to the gossip, we were bad people that didn't care about her and never visited. The decision not to see someone, even when you want to, is hard to explain to someone that has never caused their loved one to spiral into a chaotic raging mess.

Eventually, it became necessary to accept that when we visited and Grandmom became upset, we were stealing what little peace of mind she had. Taking that from her was unfair. The criticism from others made me second guess the decision more than once, even knowing I was doing what was best for her in my heart. When a loved one begins to forget you, it is hard to prevent personal ego from getting in the way of their quality of life. Demanding they remember who you are will only stress them out. Demanding recognition would have been unfair to Grandmom. Especially since her brain had already turned against her, and I didn't need to make things worse.

I have always tried to see it from Grandmom's possible perspective. I imagine she thought, "here is a very familiar person, yet a stranger, and I feel like I should know her but can't place her no matter how hard I try." Wouldn't that freak you out? I know it would scare me.

People would say to Mom, "I can't imagine my mother forgetting me; that would be so awful." Mom hoped that Grandmom would forget her. Because if Grandmom forgot her, then Mom might be able to visit her without causing unnecessary stress. Mom was the person Grandmom remembered the longest, and also the person that triggered a rage response in Grandmom. As soon as she saw Mom, even when Grandmom could not tell you Mom was her daughter, Grandmom became angry and ready to fight. Can you imagine the level of guilt that must place on someone? Even Grandmom's care team didn't understand the reaction. Eventually, Mom had to stay away too. She could stop in and check on Grandmom from a distance, but interacting wasn't always the best way to care for her.

I have interacted with many people that responded differently to their family, care team, and strangers. The different reactions are common and expected. It doesn't mean that expecting them and being prepared for the differences won't hurt when it happens. I know how hurtful it is to see a loved one be sweet to someone they don't know and then treat you like something stuck on their shoe. However, knowing something is possible and then living through it is different.

I have also witnessed people with Dementia raging against a specific family member more than once and not just within my family. Situations like this are troubling to see, but being on the receiving end of this treatment has to be worse. Each time, the person most responsible for the patient's care was the target of the rage. I have no clue why this happens, but I wish I did. Maybe then it would be easier to help others through it. No matter how many times I reassured someone it wasn't their fault, and sometimes this is just the way things are, I could still see the defeat and pain in their eyes.

Pick Your Battles

Picking your battles is a crucial part of caring for a loved one with Dementia, and we don't talk about it enough. We were constantly picking our battles with Grandmom. Even before Dementia, she wanted things her way. If it wasn't her way, then she became the most stubborn, unyielding human on the planet; at least it felt that way. The idea of picking our battles transitioned into how we addressed caring for her once she could not safely care for herself.

Dementia is the battle already chosen for you, but the others are often subjective. Disputes will differ for each person. For Grandmom, the conflicts varied daily, and what upset her one day would not bother her the next and vice versa. Again, knowing which battles are worth stressing yourself and loved ones over and which ones aren't is vital to everyone's mental health.

Grandmom was a very analytical person. She picked ideas into pieces, and Dementia did not take that away from her. However, her reasoning became less sound, making it more complicated to convince her of things. She used this method to get her way and often won because she could wear you down. It was difficult to accept that such an intelligent and rational person had lost reasoning abilities to the extent she had. And it was challenging to stop trying to reason with her. We had to stop the natural tendency to debate situations with her. We all realized it did not help the situation any, it only made things worse, but it was a hard habit to break. We had to change because Grandmom had changed.

It became a balancing act for us, what is necessary versus what is not. Once we learned to tune out the unhelpful commentary, we found that some of the battles didn't need to happen at all. Grandmom stopped caring about others' perceptions of her, and we had to learn to allow that to happen. For better or worse, she stopped noticing, and for once, she did not care about what someone might say. As long as Grandmom was not harming herself or anyone else, it was best to let it go.

There will be enough necessary battles for caregivers to fight even when they don't want to, so tuning out the unnecessary ones saves everyone from grief. Other people will often contribute to the unnecessary fights because well-meaning busybodies seek to feel better about themselves. Clothing and hair are easy to see and judge. So the way the person dresses or their hairstyle, cut, or color are easy targets for criticism by people who have no business getting involved.

Grandmom had several sisters, one of them worked as an aid for another resident at the assisted living facility. This sister constantly nagged about what Mom was doing wrong yet never tried to improve any situation. Grandmom's sister was caught on several occasions deliberately agitating Grandmom and then feigning ignorance about why Grandmom was upset. Some of these agitating events included the sister trying to force Grandmom to wear clothing that she did not want to wear. Grandmom's choice of attire became a source of contention.

Grandmom never liked anything around her neck and would swear that it was choking her. The dislike included shirts, necklaces, scarves, and any other item that touched her neck. As her cognitive function decreased, the belief she was choking increased. She would only wear tops with very wide necklines, and if an item she owned did not have a loose neck, she cut it off. By the time she moved to assisted living, most of her shirts were missing collars. Grandmom's sister took the matter of attire very personally.

The sister was highly offended that Grandmom cut the collars from her shirts and was less stylish than in years past. It became a source of contention between the sister and my mother. The sister felt Mom allowed Grandmom to dress in tatters because Mom didn't care about Grandmom. Each time the subject came up, the sister said, "what will everyone think?" Concern about others' perceptions was common among all of Grandmom's sisters. Maybe it was a generational concern, but not one shared by the rest of us. Mom felt the sister should mind her own business and let Grandmom decide what she wanted to wear.

Many choices do not include resident input in a communal setting, even assisted living. Choosing what to wear did not hurt anyone, so we all wanted to give Grandmom a choice, no matter how strange the outfit. No one in the assisted living community cared that Grandmom wore shirts she had altered. When Grandmom was comfortable and happy with her clothing, she was pleasant to the staff members and fellow residents. However, when forced into wearing anything she didn't want to wear, it was unpleasant for everyone who interacted with her.

Yet, Grandmom's sister disregarded all of this information. Other peoples' opinions held higher value than Grandmom's peace of mind and overall contentment. She demanded that Mom discard all ragged clothing and replace it with undamaged items. Grandmom's sister failed to realize that buying new clothing did not work because Grandmom didn't recognize it and gave it away or threw it in the trash. If she kept a newly purchased item for some reason, the first thing she did was cut or tear the neckline out. It was best to let Grandmom keep what she recognized and felt comfortable wearing. The resulting fights from forcing her to dress a specific way were not worth it.

Another issue with clothing ensued when Grandmom decided she did not like wearing bras. I understand where grandmom was coming from on this one. I don't know many women who like wearing bras, so I appreciate her feelings about not wanting to wear them. But we did have to know what happened to them. Because sometimes Dementia makes it imperative to ask follow-up questions and find what happened to an item. Is it just a desire to be rid of uncomfortable clothing, or has something else happened?

When an aide helping Grandmom prepare for the day mentioned the lack of bras, Grandmom said they were all stolen. The aide thought perhaps they had been lost in the wash and reported the lack of bras to Mom. Mom took a few more of Grandmom's bras from her clothing at home to the assisted living facility, and they too were soon stolen. Grandmom generally replied that someone had stolen it when asked about the missing things. The explanation of stolen became a trend, and items disappeared when Grandmom did not like them. As Grandmom's memory worsened, she automatically said someone had stolen it anytime she misplaced something, even before moving into assisted living.

Realistically it is not uncommon for women to stop wearing restrictive bras in these settings. I promise this battle was not and is not worth fighting. I don't always wear a bra at home, and this was now her home. I still see no problem with her not wearing a bra. However, Grandmom's sister once again was appalled that she went braless, and because Grandmom had said someone stole the bras, her sister took that as the gospel truth and started accusing staff of theft. Once again, creating an incident out of a non-event. While I accept that some care facilities have incidents with items truly being stolen from vulnerable residents, legitimate theft was not the case here. In this situation, it was only items that Grandmom disliked, shirts with collars, anything too tight, and this time, it was her bras.

Grandmom had never held on to anything that she did not like. The staff found most of the *stolen* items in another location within the facility; she would take them from her room and leave them somewhere else. The staff members collected the stolen things. Then they kept them until Mom visited to take the items back home or returned them to Grandmom's room, only to find them elsewhere later. However, the bras were just gone, they were not found elsewhere in the facility, and they were not in her trash. So, where did they go? And if it isn't a battle we were willing to fight, and none of us cared whether she wore a bra or not, why do we care where the bras went? Because Grandmom continued to get increasingly creative in how she disposed of items she no longer wanted.

She began throwing items from her second-story window. The landscapers gathered the things and returned them to the front office. It made their jobs harder; thankfully, they were understanding. Eventually, Grandmom's window had to be permanently locked because the staff and care team were concerned that she would attempt to climb out. The fire marshal did not initially approve of blocking the window closed. There were concerns about evacuating her during an emergency. Well, I hated to be the bearer of bad news, but in case of a fire, they couldn't have gotten her out the window anyway. There is no scenario where she could have safely exited through a window. Grandmom was in her eighties with severe osteoporosis and kyphosis; it wasn't happening. Besides, her apartment was close to an emergency exit, which was realistically the only safe way to evacuate her.

Grandmom also started flushing things down the toilet. Mostly, smaller items like washcloths and socks. I have no clue what prompted flushing items instead of throwing them into the trash, nor why the desire to flush non-flushable items becomes a thing. But this tendency happens more often than I expected and with more people than just Grandmom. No matter the setting, whether communal living or at-home care, flushing non-flushable items wreaks havoc on the plumbing. It was a surprise the first time it happened because this behavior gets overlooked or not openly discussed. Even though I knew this behavior occurred, it was upsetting when it was my grandmother. It was another glaring reminder she was changing, and the person I knew was slipping away.

This creative disposal behavior is why finding the bras was high on the priority list for the caregivers. It wasn't because Grandmom needed to wear a bra. Nor was it because she had disposed of them. The concern was in the manner Grandmom may have disposed of them. It turns out the bras were just another testament that she maintained her creativity. In this case, Grandmom had strategically hidden them. She carefully removed all face tissues from a tissue box, placed a bra or two in the bottom, and returned the tissues to the original box. I find myself wondering if the events around the bra were related to Dementia or a stroke of pure genius.

Sometimes you still have to fight a battle you would rather not, and it is easy to become agitated and even angry during these times. Our loved ones with Dementia may have some strange behavioral changes. It may feel like they are doing things to push your buttons deliberately. But I promise they aren't. As the ability to reason declines, the impulse to act overrides their normal behavior. Grandmom's changing behavior wasn't personal, even when it felt that way, and there were times it felt deliberate.

Some changes were so mind-blowing that they required time to process. Grandmom was a bit prudish. Generally, if she saw a scantily dressed person, her eyebrows would jump into her hairline, and you could see the judgment. She didn't have to say anything; her facial expression said it all. As her cognitive abilities declined, some of her inhibitions declined. Less self-consciousness isn't a characteristic unique to Grandmom. I have seen far too many family members surprised by their loved ones' sudden shift in inhibitions. The disbelief and shock in the statements of "they would never" or "I can't believe" are common. I found myself saying these same things, only to realize later that she did and would again. Because Grandmom was changing, through no fault of her own, the faster we adjusted, the better off we would all be.

Grandmom's belief that her clothing was strangling her never stopped. She did not reach a point where she ever stopped noticing high necklines on anything she had on. This sensation of strangling included hospital gowns. The nursing staff insisted Grandmom put on a hospital gown instead of her clothing during the visit. Grandmom refused to wear the gown with the opening in the back because she swore she was smothering. Instead, Grandmom turned the opening to the front and refused to tie the gown. No matter how often Mom or the staff tried to convince her to turn it around, it did not happen. Grandmom won that argument, finally wearing the hospital staff and Mom down with her obstinance.

They wanted to keep Grandmom for observation. Mom handled the administrative side of the visit, provided information for Grandmom's care, and then returned home. She hoped Grandmom would calm down for the hospital staff once Mom was out of sight. This particular emergency room had glass walls with curtains for privacy when needed. Mom's theory worked and failed all at the same time. Grandmom did calm down, and the nurses and doctor continued with their other duties. However, when Mom returned to check on Grandmom, she found a very calm Grandmom was standing in the middle of her ER cubical, completely naked. Grandmom wasn't the least bit fazed by the knowledge that the entire ER could see her like this. She said she couldn't breathe and needed air. Her need to breathe and not be smothered overrode her comprehension that she flashed everyone within the ER.

This behavior was out of character on so many levels, but there isn't anything to do. There was judgment and hand-wringing from people outside of the situation because Grandmom was naked in the ER. But those people were not there to help get her into the hospital gown. I understand that Grandmom would not have typically allowed strangers to see her naked. She would have been embarrassed, but I chose not to feel secondary embarrassment for what should've, could've, or would've been. The potential and possible were overruled by what was. There is no reason to beat yourself up. Grandmom's Dementia made her different. We had to learn to navigate those changes rather than try and reinforce the older behaviors.

Ideally, the ER is a public place, so trying to coax her into some clothing was preferred to full-on nakedness. However, the hospital staff did not seem overly concerned about her lack of clothing. Again, we are often more uncomfortable and shocked than the professionals. They have probably seen more and expect a certain level of unexpected. I encourage everyone to believe the professionals when they tell you it is okay and your loved one isn't doing anything atypical of their situation.

Even though I tried to approach Grandmom's changing mind with a belief to expect the unexpected, some things that happened were still surprising. It became necessary to address and try to stop some things that happened. The behavior wasn't only impacting her but others around her. Grandmom's ability to recognize credible threats declined along with her reasoning skills. I believe that some of her more extreme behaviors resulted from this decline.

    Grandmom started biting people.

Imagine getting a call from a care team or other family members that your elderly relative had begun biting anyone that pissed her off. Like it or not, Dementia chose this battle for us, and it was one we had no option but to fight. Any time self-harm or harm to others is involved, the opportunity to leave the person alone or let them have their way goes out the window. As Grandmom's mind deteriorated, many of her behaviors were similar to those of a young child. The difference between having a toddler that bites and a patient with Dementia biting is the inability to remember. The toddler will eventually recognize that biting is unacceptable and learn to communicate differently. The person with Dementia may or may not remember from one instance to the next, and it can be an ongoing battle.

Grandmom bit people for several months. The biting was inconsistent behavior. We never really knew what would trigger her to bite someone. The inconsistency made it nearly impossible to avoid those incidents. We began warning people that Grandmom may bite. Isn't that a horrific warning to provide for a loved one? Any new caregivers and visitors had to be warned that she may bite them and to be on guard if she bared her teeth at you. The biting was primal, millennia of human evolution forgotten. Grandmom relied on what she had and returned to the most basic manner of self-protection.

Others will most likely judge you if your loved one develops this characteristic; ignore them! Perhaps I was too unconcerned with the biting behavior, but I can see why Grandmom used it; fighting back made sense. I believe Grandmom began biting because she was afraid. Imagine waking up every day in an unfamiliar environment surrounded by strangers. She couldn't leave or go anywhere without those strangers following her and watching her. Fight the battle and accept that there is no winning. Behaviors like this happen, don't abuse yourself because you can't fix it.

Historically, I have not liked every person I ever worked with or had roommates I was not fond of, and Grandmom was the same. It is naive to think that all residents will always get along, and no one in my family expected that to be the case. Still, I was surprised how many other families expect this unrealistic fantasy. During her stay at assisted living, Grandmom went to meals with the other residents in the dining facility. Facilities like this allow residents to develop friendships and interact, especially during meals. In some situations, this creates clique groups, and some residents take where they sit during meals very seriously. It is like high school all over again.

On one occasion, another resident decided Grandmom had taken her seat in the dining room. The resident grabbed Grandmom by the arm to pull her out of the chair. The thing is, Grandmom was strong, her mind might have been in decline, but her body was strong. Grandmom pulled away from the other resident. The other resident, who was less stable on her feet, fell to the floor in the process. She fell hard and started yelling that Grandmom had pushed her down. Thankfully some staff members had witnessed the exchange and said all Grandmom did, was pull away from the other resident. It wasn't her fault the other person fell, and the other resident should not have tried to grab her or pull Grandmom from her seat.

No one is to blame in a situation like this. Of course, an older person falling or getting pulled over is not ideal, but grabbing at another person is also unacceptable. Even before she had Dementia, Grandmom wouldn't have tolerated someone trying to drag her out of a seat. Sometimes it is hard to remember that just because they have gotten older does not mean they stopped having personalities and opinions. If we don't like everyone we deal with every day, why do we forget they probably won't?

Each resident will have different needs and concerns, and all of this collectively keep the staff members on their toes. You may know what is best for your loved one, or you may not, but they are generally trying their best to make life worthwhile for all residents. Your loved one may not be the only cause for drama in a communal living setting. Just prepare for this because sometimes they will be at fault, and sometimes they aren't.

I will say this repeatedly; there is no perfect solution or exact care plan. Caring for and preventing harm for loved ones with Dementia is a process of doing the best you can with the information available at that specific time. Information will change often, and the best we can do will change just as frequently. It is an ongoing guessing game. What will work one day may not work the next, but it will work again next week. Accepting Grandmom's changes was hard, and it was odd which changes bothered me the most. I had to learn how to understand those changes and acknowledge that they impacted each family member differently.

Pouring from an Empty Cup

Being a caregiver is not an easy task. Not everyone can be a caregiver, and I promise I am one of those in the not capable category. I know my limits and embrace them. We are not all created to do the same things or have the same skillsets. I have many strengths, and one of those strengths is the sense to know that being a long-term care provider is not a personal strength. Guess what? It is perfectly okay to seek help caring for a loved one, especially if you know you aren't good at it.

It is imperative to do honest self-assessment and recognize personal limits. We can't pour from an empty cup. If we have nothing left to give, we are ineffective care providers to everyone, including ourselves. Sometimes there is nothing left to give, yet we still try, which doesn't work, leading to burnout or, worse, apathy. Caring for parents and grandparents can be an emotionally charged situation. The reversal of roles makes an already complicated dynamic more complex. My family often found ourselves at odds over what we wanted to do versus realistic capabilities. This struggle is why every non-professional person involved in the loved one's care needs to conduct an internal assessment, focusing on the difference between wants, expectations, and capability.

There is a belief that when we care for someone, we become personally responsible for providing care. The misconception is that the only acceptable method for caring for a loved one is through hands-on, highly involved interaction. While caring for others is a good idea and indeed a humanitarian thing to do. Too often, this belief becomes twisted. The thought turns into a lack of care or love if you aren't taking on all of the responsibility personally. This convoluted idea needs to stop.

I knew that caregiving wasn't a strength of mine; I was capable of understanding that personal hands-on care didn't guarantee the best care. Care takes on many shapes and forms, including stepping away.

Even when armed with that knowledge, there was still tremendous guilt and shame because we chose to move Grandmom into assisted living. It's probably normal to feel remorse when making these decisions for a loved one. Grandmom had made her wishes known. In the event she reached this point, we had specific instructions. It still felt like we were taking her choices away because she couldn't remember those previous instructions. Too often, people feel shame for not taking care of their loved ones personally or because they sought professional help. The truth is that no one should feel shame for finding a way for everyone involved to continue living their best life.

There is no perfect decision for every situation and no step-by-step textbook answers. Each decision will have benefits, problems, risks, and rewards. As long as decisions are attempts to improve the loved one's quality of life, no one should be ashamed of their choice. Knowing ourselves and answering the hard questions truthfully is one of the better ways to identify strengths and weaknesses as caregivers. Sometimes the best thing for a loved one is to be with caregivers that are not so close to the situation that events seem personal.

With Grandmom's Dementia battle, patterns emerged after the fact. There was rapid cognitive decline and then years of stability, then another rapid decline and several years without change. However, by the time the patterns emerged, they only helped us understand how events developed. Finding a routine after the fact does not help prevent or prepare for future incidents. We knew Grandmom was approaching a point where she could no longer live independently. We began discussing what to do for her and helping her choose. We identified several viable but impractical options.

At one point, Grandmom demanded Mom come live with her. However, my step-dad wasn't supposed to come. Within the span of that single conversation, Grandmom abruptly changed her mind. She swore she had never said Mom should come to live with her and was angry Mom would even consider leaving my step-dad at their house alone.

Grandmom was also unwilling to have anyone stay with her or even allow a part-time assistant for meals, medication, or cleaning. Grandmom was adamant about not allowing strangers in her home to steal from her. She became increasingly paranoid over the years. Some seemed normal aging and irritability, but it later became problematic with continued independent living.

Mom felt she had to move my Grandmom into their house. Grandmom vetoed the move. She was offended that any of us would expect her to "move into that." If it wasn't her house, it was a dump in her eyes. What were we thinking? Clearly, we were trying to harm her or swindle her somehow.

On several occasions before the Dementia took hold completely, Grandmom debated moving to the local assisted living facility. She would always talk herself out of it with the argument, "What about my stuff?" She felt like she would have to give up too many personal possessions, and she liked her stuff! The move into assisted living could have been less stressful if we had overcome that obstacle when she had a stronger memory. Then she could have participated in the decision, and perhaps the environment would have at least felt familiar. Instead, Grandmom dealt with increased confusion when the move happened. Even though she expressed the desire to move numerous times before and had written it out as a desired care plan, in the end, she did not get to decide for herself. Grandmom did not get the final say in where or when she moved.

Grandmom had been at a level state for a few years; then came the decline where she became dangerous to herself. She tried to keep everyone out of her house, refused food and did not eat consistently, refused medicine controlled by anyone else, and could no longer make decisions about personal safety. We were navigating how to take away her car and pushing for her to choose the move into assisted living. But, all of the options seemed impossible with it not being Grandmom's idea. We knew there would be a battle, and none of the alternatives seemed practical. Each presented different challenges, and we all were preparing for a confrontation. Then she wrecked. There was no more opportunity or time for discussion; the only option was to act.

Mom was not ready to take away Grandmom's freedom to make her own decisions. Taking control away from a parent isn't easy. If your parents have always made the decisions about their life, then taking that away is hard. It was impossible for Mom, and she became frozen in an unhealthy cycle, unable to take away Grandmom's autonomy. It was not an easy task to take Mom's control of the situation away either. Choosing Mom's health and wellbeing over Grandmom's was never a situation I predicted facing.

But the fact is that Grandmom was abusive to Mom. In many ways, Grandmom was a typical 1950s parent. She had no problem describing how she disciplined her kids just like everyone else; jerking, smacking, and yelling were cultural norms for disciplining children. But in addition, Grandmom was verbally and emotionally abusive. She did not see the things she said and did as abuse. Still, there is no situation where threatening to kill yourself to manipulate another person is okay.

Manipulation and emotional abuse were how Grandmom controlled Mom. Even during the worst of her Dementia, Grandmom could still manipulate people to get her way. It would have been fascinating to observe if my family hadn't been the one in chaos. The manipulation, guilt, and subsequent abuse when Grandmom didn't get her way sent Mom's blood pressure to dangerous levels from stress and anxiety. I was heartbroken and could only watch as Mom figured out that she had lived with abuse from Grandmom throughout her entire life.

I don't know if Grandmom remembered she could control Mom and get her way through guilt. Or if the guilt trip was such an integral part of their relationship that it was automatic, like breathing. But when Grandmom couldn't recall why she was at assisted living or remember it was initially her idea, she took spitefulness to an all-new level. Grandmom's demanding nature began to impact Mom's health. Mom's anxiety level went through the roof, and her blood pressure went along with it. I started making suggestions and decisions about Grandmom's health based on the impact on Mom's health.

Grandmom had always been a demanding and internally focused older person. Once Grandmom's reasoning abilities decreased to a certain point, the challenging aspects of her personality gave way to constant demands. Demands we could never possibly meet, she was unmanageable. The berating, raging, near-constant verbal abuse was killing my mother. I do not say this lightly, and I do not say this as an exaggeration for dramatic effect. I honestly thought Grandmom would outlive Mom. And to make matters worse, Grandmom's sister jumped on the bandwagon, creating strife whenever possible, agitating Grandmom into a complete meltdown, and then acting confused by the fallout. The entire process of caring for another person becomes even more draining with relatives like that; don't be that relative.

Ultimately, I took Mom's choice away too. I chose Mom's wellbeing over Grandmom's, and I am not the least bit sorry I did. I told my step-dad that Mom could not allow Grandmom to live with them under any circumstances; allowing Grandmom to live with them would be the end of Mom. She may have felt guilty about Grandmom going to assisted living, but the stress of living with Grandmom would have killed her. No matter how much guilt or obligation there is, no one should ever have to provide round-the-clock care for someone that abuses them.

My step-dad took the blame to protect me from how hurt and angry Mom became. I had begged him to push for the move to assisted living rather than bringing Grandmom home. Mom was not mentally ready to listen to options about specific actions. Mom felt like she should bring Grandmom to her house because a loving child would do that. The guilt and outside expectations were eating her up. Those well-meaning people who like to give opinions without solutions were full of how Mom should take care of Grandmom. So, he told Mom he didn't want Grandmom to live with them.

I understand that in this scenario, I'm the bully. I come by that trait honestly; I inherited it from Grandmom. I am also at peace with my actions to push the decision to the inevitable conclusion. Even though Mom was angry when it all happened and felt she didn't get a choice. Mom also knows that I convinced my stepdad to take his stance on Grandmom moving in with them. She has forgiven us both. Sometimes it isn't easy to make another person see how burnt out they are. We overestimate how much we are realistically capable of doing when caring for loved ones.

Family dynamics can make this an even more complicated process. Each of us has our connection to the loved one and will do things differently. Differences are perfectly reasonable as long as everyone tries to make life better for the loved one. Adapting to Dementia is also necessary for everyone involved. For my family, Grandmom's history of depression and her tendency to fight first made professional care the only safe option for dealing with Dementia. Her company manners were such a significant part of her personality that she was generally less combative with her care team. Decreased hostile interactions allowed her to have a more pleasant life overall.

Another reason I needed not to be a caregiver in this situation stems from inheriting some of Grandmom's less desirable traits. I am not the most empathetic person and have minimal tolerance for manipulation or emotional abuse. Enough abuse and criticism, and I become apathetic towards the person dishing it out. Knowing and accepting this truth about myself has been a struggle. I want to be a truly selfless person, but I am not. I am fascinated by completely selfless people. I say this because apathy doesn't just occur in people like me.

For caregivers, apathy can come from burnout. Being drained and emotionally worn out can also create feelings of apathy. Again, you have nothing left to give, and you can't even care about not having it. This feeling is dangerous in a caregiver situation. Professionals experience burnout too, but they have also learned different coping mechanisms because of their field of work. When it is family, and you live it day in and day out, it comes on before you may even recognize what is happening to you. I saw burnout in Mom before she did. Mom's declining health was an indicator of how severe burnout can impact a person. There is nothing wrong with getting help.

Additionally, no one deserves to be abused physically, emotionally, or in any other manner. Both caregivers and the person receiving care are worthy of respect and support. If you ever find yourself in a situation where you must become a caregiver to someone that has abused or is currently abusive to you, please seek outside help. Seek out the professionals because, with Dementia, the behavior could become worse. Professional care and external caregivers are sometimes a more practical approach to protecting everyone's emotional well-being.

We Need Help! Now What?

My family knew long before we sought help what Grandmom's wishes were because she had made them clear on several occasions, using multiple methods, even writing instructions in one of the many Bibles. However, knowing her wishes and us carrying them out was more complex. Not all care facilities will accept residents with Dementia. The inability to provide a safe environment is often a factor in the facility's acceptance or rejection of a resident. This evaluation criterion is most common within assisted living communities. Specialized care is also why some facilities can't take people with specific care needs. Generalization is common among care facilities. Some conditions require a care facility designed to provide the best care for that medical need.

There are several types of care providers. There are benefits to each kind of care, and no single style will be the exact fit for every person. Talking through the scenarios and knowing our loved one's preferences is essential. It may seem morbid and can be an awkward conversation, but it is still necessary. The most common care providers include home health, assisted living, skilled nursing, and nursing homes. I choose to break skilled nursing and nursing homes into two categories; others lump them together. My method of distinguishing the different facilities is a preference, not a mandate, because some facilities fall into more than one category. Regardless of the option chosen, some specialized treatment or doctor's appointments may require the person to visit another location.

Home Health offers a wide variety of services at all skill levels. This category is outstanding if it is medically possible for the person to remain in their home. Home health was the preferred option for my grandparents on the other side of my family. Care started with a nurse stopping by to drop off meds and take vitals. Additionally, the physical and respiratory therapists came to the home for treatments. Eventually, their care became more extensive and transitioned to palliative care. But they never had to move into a hospital setting. Going into a hospital was not what either wanted to do, and both were more comfortable remaining at home.

Assisted living communities are more like home health but at a facility. Some Assisted living facilities may look more like free-standing communities. In contrast, others will look like apartments or condos attached to communal facilities. This facility style offers more opportunities for residents to continue living independently with minor assistance. There is the comfort of knowing that someone is close by to help them if they need assistance. Often assisted living communities are about peace of mind for the residents. The individual residences within the community may have a full kitchen and laundry, allowing residents to perform these activities themselves. Others may have a partial kitchen and offer the flexibility for the resident to eat meals in their rooms or the community setting. Assisted living may provide residents with services unique to their specific needs, including light housekeeping or laundry. These are flexible care facilities.

Skilled nursing facilities and nursing homes are very similar; both become home to the residents. Skilled nursing facilities care for people with minor to extensive medical needs. These facilities offer the residents access to full-time nursing staff. However, they also provide residents with in-house therapies, including occupational therapy, physical therapy, and speech therapy. The intention of including therapy sessions is to keep residents living their best life, with the most functionality, for as long as possible. Skilled nursing is a more intense level of care and interaction from medical providers than assisted living.

Just as with skilled nursing, residents have access to full-time care. Nursing homes care for people with more extensive medical needs. These facilities are more structured and can operate more like a hospital, including controlling the number of visitors or visitation hours. Nursing homes are a prevalent care option, and most smaller communities have at least one. Nursing homes are frequently complained about and disparaged but provide a vital service to older people with extensive medical needs. Sadly, seniors without extensive medical concerns sometimes end up in nursing homes in smaller towns and communities because of the lack of retirement communities or advocates for senior citizens.

The only facility near our hometown that Grandmom found acceptable was a lovely, assisted living community. She chose this facility years before developing Dementia. She also refused the idea of home health, she did not want an outsider in her home, and she was adamant about it. Her last house was also not a user-friendly home. It was an older house with additions that created multiple levels between every room. I was honestly glad she chose the assisted living facility.

Carrying out Grandmom's desired living

preference was made more complex by Dementia. The facility could offer the care she needed up to a certain point. This facility provided Grandmom a single-story living environment, consistent meals with appropriate nutrition, medication management, full-time access to emergency care, and general observation without intrusion. They couldn't provide a full-time assistant to manage her cognitive decline and outbursts. The facility manager was upfront about this. If Grandmom required constant supervision, we were responsible for meeting that need.

This ability to tailor care to Grandmom's needs is why I view this particular assisted living as a flexible care environment. It is not uncommon for assisted living residents to have a personal assistant or companion, paid for by their families. The staff members at this facility worked with our family to assist us in providing the best possible care for Grandmom. Because of this flexibility, even as Grandmom's cognitive abilities declined, the assisted living facility offered her choices. She slept, paced the halls, stood looking out windows, and interacted or didn't at her will. These choices would not have been possible in other types of facilities.

As Grandmom's needs increased, the number of personal companions and caregivers increased. She had three assistants to provide round-the-clock supervision and support by the end of her life. It wasn't cheap. As I said, Grandmom had picked this facility before developing cognitive problems. She worked with a financial advisor ensuring there was enough money for her to be taken care of in a manner she deemed appropriate. Grandmom made known her wants to all of us and set out to make sure it happened. She was intelligent and independent; she always said she would not be a "burden" on anyone. We were very fortunate that Grandmom made those arrangements.

Given how combative she became with the immediate family, it terrifies me to think of what our lives would have been like if we were the daily care providers. On top of the stresses keeping her at home would have created, there were things that we would have never even thought to address. Additionally, the community setting met needs we never imagined in ways we couldn't have provided at home. On the infrequent occasions that Grandmom wanted to be with others, the communal areas allowed this without the pressure of having someone in her space. Being in this facility also offered an opportunity for the staff to observe Grandmom daily in a non-agitated state.

The passive observation provided better information on the overall condition of her health and mental state.

A particular instance where the observations contributed to a better quality of life included an unusual but effective medical treatment. This observation and team assessment allowed her to receive better care than a single person's observation if she had been at home with family or home health. More eyes on her problems and behaviors ultimately allowed for more care options and information. The caregivers documented the behaviors and provided that information to Grandmom's doctor. The doctor believed that Grandmom would benefit from attention-deficit/hyperactivity disorder (ADHD) medication. Grandmom had never been diagnosed with ADHD, so this was an intriguing possibility. After all, they had exhausted almost every other traditional treatment option.

Grandmom had stopped sleeping through the night. Her routine became sleeping in very short spans, getting up and pacing the floors, and another short nap. Grandmom was always on the move. She never rested, causing her cognition problems to worsen and wearing her out physically. The lack of rest exacerbated every other symptom, significantly decreasing her quality of life. Even though the medication wouldn't alter her cognitive decline, her doctor hoped that treating some of the other concerns could improve her quality of life.

The short time Grandmom was allowed to receive this medication improved her quality of life significantly. She slept through the night, her outlook improved, and she stopped being so afraid all the time. However, Grandmom's insurance company decided that there was no way an 84-year-old could develop ADHD and refused the medication. Because the paper pushers without medical degrees thought they knew better than the doctor.

Yeah! Another battle that didn't need to happen but did because of money-grubbing idiots. Mom offered to pay out of pocket for the medication and leave the insurance company out of the process. Of course, the medicine that worked was EXPENSIVE! However, the care team, nurses, and the doctor felt they could present enough evidence to demonstrate the necessity and force the insurer to cover the medication because of that expense. The process to get the medicine back became lengthy and took considerable time. Grandmom would die before the insurance company considered covering the treatment.

Do I seem a little bitter about this? I was irate then, and I am still troubled by this event. Without the medication, her quality of life diminished rapidly. The anxiety and fearfulness returned full force. The need to constantly move came back, only sleeping in short naps again. The lack of sleep and the continual movement took a toll on her otherwise healthy physical being, leading to falls, increased illness, and general irritability. The combination of these factors created the events that led to her death.

Why is all of this important? Because we had a support team, one that we wouldn't have had otherwise. I am partial to assisted living and retirement communities, but that might not be the answer for everyone. I encourage everyone to research options. And whenever possible, make your wishes known. Grandmom did this for us, and I am so thankful she did. Because even though she no longer remembered that it was her directives, we could at least do our best to carry out what she previously asked of us.

Opinions, Everybody Has One

Every person you meet during your loved one's journey will have an opinion. And now I am going to give you mine. Do what is best for your loved one and tell everyone else to back off. Seriously! If you are doing your best and someone criticizes you or your loved one, shut them down, especially if they are not active care team members. Start from the beginning and set boundaries. Setting boundaries is beneficial because not everyone will have the loved one's best interest and quality of life in mind. There is no room for negativity, wishful thinking, or what-if scenarios when you are busy living with the reality that is Dementia.

People are helpful, and I say this in all seriousness. Most humans naturally are communal creatures, and we like helping groups with which we identify and feel a kinship. When dealing with Grandmom's Dementia, we received a lot of support from all over the place. Strangers with similar circumstances, friends, family, and community members commiserated, shared stories, provided perspectives on treatment, and offered insight into things to expect. Sometimes the support came from unexpected places, a brief discussion in waiting rooms or checkout lines.

Strangers can often be more sympathetic than family members.

I believe in being supportive when others are facing a similar situation. Sometimes, our help doesn't come across as helpful but rather as judgment. We need to learn to distinguish between helpful advice and snarky opinion. Unsolicited but practical advice includes facility information, care provider contacts, or information on who specializes in Dementia care. If there are multiple facilities in the area, is one considered the best prepared to address specific needs? Do they have staff skilled in certain services? This type of information is always welcome. This advice and information usually do not critique the family's choices. This discourse is more about providing information and less about opinions on how the family reacts.

However, the less helpful and judgmental advice did not stop. We encountered many situations requiring us to make the least unpleasant decision. This decision-making process happens so often that we can't allow uninvolved parties to destroy potential joy. Yet, even I struggled with some choices and allowed self-reproach to manifest. As a general life rule, I don't do guilt when giving my best. If my best isn't good enough for someone else, I tell them where to stick their unsolicited opinion. Choosing not to do guilt is an attitude I highly recommend when dealing with busybodies. Instead, I decided to focus on potential joy and let everything else pass by whenever possible. However, even with my attitude, some people insisted on telling me their opinions on how my family handled Grandmom.

As soon as anyone found out Grandmom had Dementia, we had a surplus of opinions on how to deal with her disease, finances, home, car, and even her will. Everyone was suddenly an expert on her business. The random extended family had opinions out of their concern for what she might leave them in her will. Her care was deemed less important than what they might get. First, she wasn't dead! Second, it is pretty presumptuous to decide you should be in someone's will. She was my grandmother, and I figured she only mentioned her daughters in the will. Because she had focused most of her energy on ensuring she received appropriate care in the worst situation. Bless her for doing that because otherwise, we would have had an even harder time carrying out her plans.

Some comments and opinions come from a misunderstanding about Dementia. I kept encountering people that thought

Dementia automatically made Grandmom sweet and biddable. I frequently had to explain to others that Grandmom wasn't the lady in the commercial who was happy someone was there to take care of her, submissive and easily managed. Grandmom forgot everything around her, but she was still the stubborn, willful woman she had always been. She wanted things her way, even if she couldn't remember what consisted of her way.

We also received criticism for the battles we chose to fight and those we didn't. No decision was ever good enough, and even strangers will tell you how wrong you are. I have pretty thick skin. Another characteristic I developed from dealing with Grandmom. But other peoples' opinions and constant criticism will wear you out. Mom got the worst of it because she was in our hometown community. It still amazes me how folks aren't shy with their judgment and seem to have no clue that their opinions aren't needed or wanted.

Each of us dealt with outside opinions in different ways. I would initially attempt to educate about the reality of Dementia and how no two people will be the same. If that didn't work, my following response was often meaner. Only a few times did it reach the point where I asked when they planned to sign up to help care for

Grandmom or how much they were contributing to her care. I am more openly like the person she was with the immediate family. I try, but I am not a nice person. My brother ignored people; when pushed, he was mean like me. Auntie tried to find peace and consideration for everyone's feelings, choosing love and light. And Mom tried all of these things with a helping of guilt.

Mom does guilty very well. Grandmom spent a lot of time telling Mom what she did wasn't good enough, even before developing Dementia. Grandmom was an exceptionally critical parent and frequently criticized her children in her grandchildren's presence. It was awkward. Yet it shows how strange life was because she was a pretty supportive grandparent. Grandmom was critical of Mom as an adult, so I can imagine how critical Grandmom had been when Mom was little. It is easy to see how constantly being told your best isn't good enough could impact caregiving. It is no wonder Mom second-guessed every action and decision and felt guilt no matter what she did.

The thing is, guilt can eat you alive. Guilt causes stress, and stress can kill you. As long as we do our best in the situation, there is no reason to feel guilty; still, it can creep into our heads. No one is perfect, and this situation does not lend itself to defined solutions. There is no ideal way to take care of a loved one with Dementia. Each person's life experiences and changing mind will create different circumstances for them and their family members. We were not just dealing with Grandmom's Dementia. We dealt with a lifetime of depression, long-term prescription medication use, some medication abuse, and an old brain injury. But outsiders did not know all of that. So there was more than enough side-eye and commenting regarding how we handled her care.

The snide comments ate Mom up. I constantly reassured Mom we were doing our best, and that is all that anyone should expect in a situation like this. If others wanted something more, I felt they should have stepped up and done more. There isn't enough time in the day to deal with the criticism people seem to toss out at families going through this struggle. That alone is emotionally exhausting.

All of this led me to a point where I try not to judge others on how they treat their family because family dynamics are often complicated. When I have judgmental thoughts about others' treatment of their parents or grandparents, I try to remind myself how others judged us. It can be hard to remember that my judgments are about my perceptions and personal interactions. Sadly, just because their relative is good to me, they may not have had the same interactions.

Our perceptions of people we deal with in a specific environment vary greatly. Think about how people can have different views about a neighbor or coworker. This difference is because not everyone receives the same treatment, and we need to recognize this when judging others. The way you see a person and your experiences with them may be drastically different than what another has experienced. Outsiders and extended family judged us very harshly for how we reacted to some of Grandmom's behaviors as the Dementia progressed. Grandmom was skilled with company manners, and she had masked her disease for a very long time. Therefore, there were a wide variety of perceptions about her and us.

When I start judging others, I find it personally effective to determine how much responsibility I am willing to take. If I feel the person has an unmet need, am I ready to meet that need? Doing this helps me identify real concerns over judgment. If I truly believe a person isn't receiving adequate care or compassion, it is my responsibility to step up. Otherwise, I am probably just being one of the well-meaning jerks.

Grief Cycle

Grief is a strange emotion, and it throws so much at you at once that sometimes it becomes almost impossible to identify the actual feelings. Have you ever been sad and laughing simultaneously? I have. There were so many conflicting emotions. At times, I felt like I was losing my grip on reality. And you know what, that is okay too. When the emotions would overtake me, I learned to step back and focus on surviving that wave. Once I felt calmness return, then I returned to focus on another problem, one at a time, day by day. Sometimes, we forget to permit ourselves to exist in survival mode for short spells. I find peace knowing that it is acceptable not to thrive or be great every once in a while, but simply survive.

A fundamental but flexible concept from Introduction to Psychology or Psych 101 includes the five stages of grief. Commonly identified as denial, anger, bargaining, depression, and acceptance, the five stages of grief are not an exact science. Sometimes, there may be a few more added or in a different order because it is a flexible idea. Not everyone moves through the stages in precisely the same manner. I tend to hit anger first, disbelief comes later in my process. There is no correct formula for processing loss as long as we process it.

However, psychology's five stages of grief did nothing to prepare me for the cyclic grieving that happened as Grandmom declined. Each change brought new loss and new grief, and there were times when the stages overlapped as something new developed. Living in a continuous cycle of grieving is exhausting. This continual state is when I learned survival mode works and stopped beating myself up over it.

I found it surprising just how many different times I grieved the loss of Grandmom. However, when she reached the end of her life, I was relieved, praying that she was finally at peace. Because by the end of her life, I had grieved her loss on too many occasions to count. I was broken-hearted when she forgot me, forgot others that she loved, and when she told me about myself. It happened over and over. It was a new experience for me, experiencing the loss of someone still living and then losing them again and again. The sadness and loss happened so many times that I was no longer capable of continuing to grieve her loss. I was exhausted.

Even as I write that small sentence, I feel guilty. How can I be so selfish that I can't continue to grieve? Admitting that I can only mourn loss so much seems selfish. Knowing my grief cycle stopped soon after her death often makes others uncomfortable, and it appears heartless. Please understand that I genuinely miss the person who had good days. Despite Grandmom's quirks and oddities, she brought so much joy when she was in good spirits. It is hard not to miss that side of her. But I grieved her loss while she was alive. Bit by bit, the person she had always been was disappearing, and there was only a shadow remaining.

It is a concept that I still have difficulty wrapping my mind around. Some believe we should have enjoyed the person Grandmom was becoming, but that is the tricky part. She wasn't becoming someone different she was losing all of her good days and happy memories. The things Grandmom found joy in were disappearing, and we caused her additional stress. We still looked familiar, she could see us in her reflection, but she didn't know us. So when we were around, any chance for a happy day was quickly gone. Perhaps it was selfish. Still, I didn't enjoy causing her additional distress.

That is one of the complex problems associated with cognitive diseases. How do we identify when we create more problems for our loved ones than we fix? We found valued members of a care team that helped us identify stressors and areas for improving life's quality. Again, there isn't a perfect outline to follow. The best I could hope was to make choices with compassion and love and learn to forgive myself.

Grandmom's journey was incredibly stressful, and I am sorry to say that your loved one may experience a similar journey. There will be ways to manage symptoms, but they will not get better. Life will create enough stress during this time. However, try to avoid focusing or dwelling on the negative. My goal was to create laughter for Grandmom and make my time with her fun, and I was always good at making her laugh.

People will tell you to be sure and visit and to create memories together. Allow me to provide a hard-to-swallow pill of truth. We were not creating memories. I was making memories, but I was only improving her life at that moment. When I was out of sight, I no longer existed for her. The grown granddaughter making her laugh was a stranger, and her granddaughter was a small child. Just accept that the memories of the things you do when your loved one is in a significant cognitive decline are yours and yours alone. Embrace them but recognize they are not shared, so trying to improve their life at that moment is about the best you can do.

Currently, no medical breakthroughs will prevent the inevitable conclusion to Dementia, and I pray this changes in the future. What a blessing a cure would be for the families that will continue to deal with this. One of the aspects of any long-term illness is to ensure the caregivers and other loved ones do not also become collateral damage of the disease. So often, the idea of being a compassionate caregiver to others leads us to forget or forgo compassion for ourselves.

Personally, the effects of continuous cycles of grief surprised me. Even though I am not a gloomy person, the ongoing grief cycle led to more prolonged bouts of depression. And yes, I am one of those people that believes everyone gets depressed, just like everyone gets happy. Humans are imperfect systems that balance our positives and negatives. During the never-ending long-term cycle, I experienced generally poorer health overall, colds, migraines, and digestive problems increased. It went on for so long I thought I was sick, but I wasn't, at least not in a diseased sense. Once the cycles slowed, the other symptoms eased.

Grandmom died on my 40th birthday. I laughed. Not because she had died but because I could see the humor in the date and knew she would have too. Everyone was quick to reassure me that she didn't do that on purpose. I think it was because everyone knew what I did, and no one wanted to broach the reality of her warped sense of humor. Grandmom was exceptionally dramatic. If she could've planned it, she would've planned it and gotten a good laugh out of the situation. Grandmom's date of passing ensured that she gets remembered as long as I live. Essentially my birthday became the anniversary of her death.

>Have I mentioned Grandmom was dramatic?

About the Author

Toni is a jack of all trades, an Army Veteran, and spouse to a career soldier. She loves learning new things and has an A.A. in Intelligence Operations, an A.A.S in Occupational Therapy Assistance, a B.B.A. in Human Resource Management, and held licenses as a massage therapist and aesthetician.

Toni loves old cars, animals, and crocheting but might have a mild problem buying more yarn than she can ever use. Toni has lived all over the United States and is still moving around. However, no matter where she roams, The Pound and the mountains of Southwestern Virginia will always be home.

Made in the USA
Columbia, SC
29 September 2024